BLUEPRINTS
The Handwriting Book

Helen Hadley

Stanley Thornes (Publishers) Ltd

Do you receive *BLUEPRINTS NEWS*?

Blueprints is an expanding series of practical teacher's ideas books and photocopiable resources for use in primary schools. Books are available for separate infant and junior age ranges for every core and foundation subject, as well as for an ever widening range of other primary teaching needs. These include **Blueprints Primary English** books and **Blueprints Resource Banks**. Blueprints are carefully structured around the demands of National Curriculum in England and Wales, but are used successfully by schools and teachers in Scotland, Northern Ireland and elsewhere.

Blueprints provide:
- *Total curriculum coverage*
- *Hundreds of practical ideas*
- *Books specifically for the age range you teach*
- *Flexible resources for the whole school or for individual teachers*
- *Excellent photocopiable sheets – ideal for assessment and children's work profiles*
- *Supreme value.*

Books may be bought by credit card over the telephone and information obtained on **(01242) 577944**. Alternatively, photocopy and return this **FREEPOST** form to receive **Blueprints News**, our regular update on all new and existing titles. You may also like to add the name of a friend who would be interested in being on the mailing list.

Please add my name to the **BLUEPRINTS NEWS** mailing list.

Mr/Mrs/Miss/Ms _____

Home address _____

_____ Postcode _____

School address _____

_____ Postcode _____

Please also send **BLUEPRINTS NEWS** to:

Mr/Mrs/Miss/Ms _____

Address _____

_____ Postcode _____

To: Marketing Services Dept., Stanley Thornes Ltd, FREEPOST (GR 782), Cheltenham, GL50 1BR

Text © Helen Hadley 1996
Original line illustrations by Atelier Illustrations © ST(P) Ltd 1996

First published in 1996 by:
Stanley Thornes (Publishers) Ltd
Ellenborough House
Wellington Street
CHELTENHAM GL50 1YW
England

A catalogue record for this book is available from the British Library.

ISBN 0–7487–1989–X

Typeset by Tech-Set, Gateshead, Tyne & Wear.
Printed and bound in Great Britain

96 97 98 99 00 / 10 9 8 7 6 5 4 3 2 1

CONTENTS

INTRODUCTION

Blueprints: The Handwriting Book makes the skill of handwriting fun and helps children to learn to write legibly and speedily. You can use it either as a scheme in itself or to support the scheme currently being used in your school. The lively and purposeful activities provide a structured development from left to right orientation and letter formation through the stages required for the development of a fluent, easy joined style. The sequence of skills taught can also be adapted to suit the needs of particular pupils in your class.

This practical book is in two parts. Part 1 offers material for the teacher and Part 2 contains 123 photocopiable sheets for the pupils. Part 1 covers factors to consider when forming a school policy: the need for a whole school policy, the needs of the teachers and the children, the requirements of the National Curriculum, decisions to be made when forming your curriculum guidelines in handwriting, practical suggestions for teaching handwriting and ways of dealing with some common problems.

The pupils' copymasters in Part 2 are divided into eight sections:

● **Section 1** has activities for developing left to right orientation, pencil control and the movements needed to form basic letter shapes.

● **Section 2** teaches single letter shapes through tracing, drawing and copying. The letters are taught in family groups so that a simple stroke can be developed to form a number of similar letters. This speeds up children's mastery by using a redundancy approach to learning. It provides copymasters for variant forms of certain letters like '**b**', '**f**', '**p**', '**s**', '**v**', '**w**' and '**y**' so that you can select the letter shape closest to your school's preferred style.

● **Section 3** introduces children to capital letters and numerals.

● **Section 4** gives practice in both diagonal and horizontal joins.

● **Section 5** gives children practice in joining letters to make words which use common letter strings and spelling useful everyday words.

● **Section 6** contains items for children to copy as handwriting practice. The pieces vary in length and range from proverbs to poems and rhymes.

● **Section 7** contains borders for children to complete and others which encourage children to display and present their writing attractively.

● **Section 8** is a collection of items. There are letter flip charts which show children how letters are written, lines to use underneath blank paper as writing guides, and letter charts.

You will find that *Blueprints: The Handwriting Book* provides a step-by-step approach to teaching handwriting. It works systematically through the stages needed for the development of a fluent, easy joined writing style in a way that is both practical and fun.

PART 1
ABOUT
HANDWRITING

A WHOLE SCHOOL POLICY

NEEDS ▶

The school

The whole school needs to follow the same approach in order to maintain continuity of learning. This is vitally important in the infant school because it is here that the basis of a child's handwriting style is set for many years to come. The more energy that is put into teaching handwriting at this level the less time is required later on. Clear guidance must be given if children are to learn to write well.

These are some of the priorities which should direct our thinking when considering a school style:

- writing needs to be legible so that it is easy to read
- it must be clear, speedy to execute and in a flowing easy style
- the style taught at the beginning must be one which leads easily and naturally to a joined style and is suited to a number of writing needs
- the model should be a cursive one because even when it is not joined it is faster to write than print script
- there must be clear guidelines so that there is continuity when pupils progress from one class to the next
- it must be well taught from the start because writing is a skill which is to serve the learner throughout his or her lifetime.

The teachers

All teachers need a good knowledge of how to teach handwriting from the early motor skills and left to right orientation through to correct letter strokes, joins and the stages required to develop a fluent, easy writing style. They need also to be aware of the letter construction faults and pencil grip some new school entrants will have developed elsewhere and seek to remedy them when introducing them to the school's chosen style. They also need to know how to solve common problems.

The onus of teaching the beginnings of good handwriting lies with the reception class teacher because it is here at the start of formal education that the correct pencil grip, posture and letter formation should be formed. If handwriting is taught well during a pupil's infant years all that should be needed afterwards is a general refresher at the beginning of each new school year; any particular faults should be dealt with on an individual basis. Primary teachers need clear guidelines and an understanding of the processes involved to help their pupils acquire a flowing, natural, personal hand which will enable them to cope with the pressures of today's secondary education.

The children

All children need to be taught a basic, fundamental model at the beginning from which they can develop their own personal style. They need to develop one which is clear, fluent and easy to write and one which they can write quickly enough to get down what they want to say while it is still in their heads. They need to be taught in a logical way so that they can see how the learning of one letter can be used as the basis for learning another. They also need to be taught in a relaxed way so that anxiety does not spoil their work or cause muscular tensions which can lead to problems at a later date.

Blueprints: The Handwriting Book supplies these needs with a clear, step-by-step model for teaching handwriting.

AN ESSENTIAL SKILL ▶

The importance of handwriting

Most teachers would agree that writing is an essential, even crucial, skill for children to acquire. Not only is it a necessary means of communication but, socially, poor handwriting is a real disadvantage. The inability to write clearly is often associated with limited intellectual ability; work can be judged by its appearance rather than its content. Good handwriting, however, can make the difference between passing and failing examinations and being successful in job applications. Children need to develop a neat and legible style so that their writing can be read and accepted.

It is not difficult to acquire a good handwriting style provided that it is taught well from the beginning. Habitual wrong movements are harder to correct. *Blueprints: The Handwriting Book* will help to provide the foundation for a clear, speedy and flowing style of handwriting, with the correct movements being taught right from the start.

Legibility and speed

All handwriting is intended to be read but the purpose and audience can vary. Different standards apply when we scribble notes for ourselves, or use writing to think or plan rather than when we present formal work for others to read. Not all work needs to be written in one's best handwriting. Children's creative writing must not be slowed by demanding that each piece of work is perfectly written but there are times, when the finished work needs to be presented as part of a display or as a gift to others, when only one's best possible writing is good enough.

Legibility, rather than perfection, should be the first priority. Handwriting should be easy to read, evenly spaced and evenly written. It should be able to be written swiftly for notes and lists and should be clear, readable and quick for letters and most school work. It should also be capable of being used as an art form for display, presentation and those very special occasions.

Speed is the second priority. Children need to write quickly enough to complete their writing tasks or assignments, especially in tests and examinations, so that what they know and are able to express can be accurately assessed. When it comes to speed, print is no match for cursive writing. Learning the correct movements from the beginning helps to develop the necessary fast, smooth and flowing hand.

A sense of pride

Pleasure and satisfaction in being able to make the right marks on paper need to be maintained. Two-year-olds are excited about what happens when they scribble a writing implement across a piece of paper because, as if by magic, marks come out of the action and make unbelievable changes to the blank sheet of paper. An element of control is achieved over time and the marks begin to be the ones the children intend to make. They begin to write their name and copy words like 'love from' in a birthday card. Those around them are proud of their achievements – and then they come to school…
We need to retain the excitement, the magic, of making marks on paper and give it reason, sense and purpose. We want the children to develop their skills and keep their sense of pride in their growing skills and achievements.

Children need to see for themselves that their control over their handwriting is growing and to remain enthusiastic about it. A folder of their work, dated, will give evidence to them (and interested others) that progress is being made. They should be able to use their handwriting for labelling maps and diagrams, for finished work or for making notes. They need to feel that their work is good enough to show to others and is not hidden away between the covers of an exercise book. Their work should be displayed in and around the school for others to see, used to advertise school events and productions, their handwritten stories made up in book form and put in the book corner, in other classes as well as their own, along with picture story books they have made for the youngest children. Their letters should be posted, written messages delivered and, when they are old enough, they should write short notes and letters home to their parents themselves, in a careful joined script, rather than always taking home photocopied ones. Writing has to have both sense and purpose if it is seen to be a valuable skill and worth the time spent learning it.

What are we trying to achieve?

Simply put we want children to have command over the medium so that they can write down what they want to say speedily and legibly. To do this we must teach children a handwriting style which will be an asset to them throughout their school and working life. Handwriting is the means by which we express and present our thoughts, opinions and ideas but it is also the means by which we are judged.

In the first instance we want children to develop fine motor skills and left to right directionality. We also want them to recognise and use the different letter strokes and movements necessary to develop a fast, flowing joined style.

We want them to form their letters correctly so that their writing is easy to read and to make joins which are swift and simple to execute. The formation of letters and joins must become so automatic that children do not have to think about how to form them. They must be free to focus on what they want to write. Practise brings improved motor control which, in turn, brings this freedom.

How do we know if we have been successful? Simply keep samples of children's work during the time they are with you and compare them. Watch them working and you will see them becoming more confident in what and how they write.

As children gain control over the medium, legibility and speed increase. Handwriting becomes a functional tool but we do need to watch that legibility is not sacrificed in favour of speed.

THE NATIONAL CURRICULUM

The discussion and suggestions in Part 1 and the activities in Part 2 of *Blueprints: The Handwriting Book* lead children naturally through the stages required by the National Curriculum for English. We stress the need for clear, legible handwriting, and that children's writing style should be comfortable. Activities reinforce: left to right orientation; the need to start and finish letters correctly; the regularity of size and shape of letters; the regular spacing of letters and words. Children are helped to develop a clear and fluent cursive style which is neat and legible and able to be adapted to a range of tasks.

GENERAL REQUIREMENTS FOR ENGLISH KEY STAGES 1–4

1. English should develop pupils' abilities to communicate effectively in speech and writing and to listen with understanding.

● To develop as effective writers, pupils should be taught to use:
● presentational skills – accurate punctuation, correct spelling and legible handwriting.

WRITING

Key Stage 1
1. Range
a Pupils should be helped to understand the value of writing as a means of remembering, communicating, organising and developing ideas and information, and as a source of enjoyment. Pupils should be taught to write independently on subjects that are of interest and importance to them.

2. Key Skills
e In **handwriting**, pupils should be taught to hold a pencil comfortably in order to develop a legible style which follows the conventions of written English, including:

● writing from left to right across the page and from the top to the bottom of the page;
● starting and finishing letters correctly;
● regularity of size and shape of letters;
● regularity of spacing of letters and words.

They should be taught the conventional ways of forming letters, both lower case and capitals. They should build on their knowledge of letter formation to join letters in words. They should develop an awareness of the importance of clear and neat presentation, in order to communicate their meaning effectively.

Key Stage 2
2. Key Skills
e In **handwriting**, pupils should be given opportunities to continue to develop legible handwriting in both joined up and printed styles. As pupils become increasingly confident and independent, they should be encouraged to develop greater control and fluency. They should be taught to use different forms of handwriting for different purposes, *e.g. print for labelling maps or diagrams; a clear, neat hand for finished, presented work; a faster script for notes.*

5

ATTAINMENT TARGETS ▶

Level Descriptions

By the end of Key Stage 1, the performance of the great majority should be within the range of Levels 1 to 3, by the end of Key Stage 2 it should be within the range 2 to 5.

Attainment target 3: writing

Level 1   Letters are usually clearly shaped and correctly oriented.

Level 2   In handwriting, letters are accurately formed and consistent in size.

Level 3   Handwriting is joined and legible.

Level 4   Handwriting is fluent, joined and legible.

Level 5   Handwriting is joined, clear and fluent, and, where appropriate, is adapted to a range of tasks.

NATIONAL CURRICULUM REQUIREMENTS – SCOTTISH ▶

Attainment targets: handwriting and presentation

Level A – In the writing tasks above, form letters and space words legibly for the most part.

Level B – In the writing tasks above, form letters and space words legibly in linked script.

Level C – In the writing tasks above, employ a fluent, legible style of handwriting.

Writing

Handwriting skills will be formally taught, especially in the early years. Later, pupils will pay attention to handwriting in the normal course of composing their own writing.

Writing: handwriting and presentation

Level A

Pupils will spend much time drawing and using material to develop hand–eye co-ordination. Pupils will be introduced systematically to letter formation and word spacing. Spacing will be reinforced by reading and pupils will be shown how spacing helps the reader and that it will help their own writing. At an appropriate stage, linkage of letters will be taught.

Level B/C

The process of development will continue, with the aim being to help pupils build up an easy flow which will not hamper the train of thought. The teacher will take time to ensure that pupils lay out and present their writing in a neat, legible form which aids the reader. The eventual outcome will be that the pupil can consistently employ a fluent, legible style of handwriting. Pupils with difficulties in handwriting, arising, for example, from lack of motor control, will produce attractive writing and gain in confidence through the use of word-processing.

When taking a fresh look at your existing guidelines or planning new ones there are certain issues to be considered and a number of questions to be asked. Look through the handwriting schemes currently on the market and decide:

- the writing style to be adopted
- the specific letter forms to be used
- the height of letters in relation to each other
- whether exit and/or entry strokes will be used
- how letters will be joined
  letters which change shape
  which letters should not be joined

- the terminology to be used
- the standard of writing acceptable in different situations.

Other points you need to consider include:

- the three P's – pencil, paper, posture
- whether to use lines
- practical aspects of teaching handwriting
- assessment and record keeping
- working with left-handers
- dealing with problems.

All of these issues are discussed below.

HANDWRITING ISSUES

Choice of style

The model ultimately selected has to be as close to the teachers' preferred style as possible because they have to teach it. Once a model is adopted by the school, however, it must be taken on board by new teachers so as to provide pupils with a consistent approach.

To print or not to print is a core issue in making this decision. The argument for print is that children live in a world where print surrounds them. What actually surrounds them are all kinds of lettering, not just print. The lettering they see differs in size, shape, style, colour and legibility.

Printing is not like real writing it is stop-start, laborious, it doesn't flow and it is slow. It does not lead easily to joining, the learned motor movements which quickly become automatic condition the hand to stop at the line. Consequently it takes much longer to develop the flow needed for joined writing than if the child had been taught to use exit strokes from the beginning. Any attempt to teach the flowing movements needed for joined writing alongside print script confuses the child utterly because the two are so opposed. A cursive style with exit strokes provides a good foundation for joined writing and is the one chosen for *Blueprints: The Handwriting Book.*

Which specific letter forms should be used?

You need to consider whether the style should teach round or oval letter shapes and whether the letters should be slanted or upright. The letter forms preferred by teachers are often governed by the style which has become their own practised hand over the years. A number of letters, such as 'b', 'f', 'k', 'p', 'v' and 'w', have more than one form. These are often referred to as mutant letters because of the way the changes have developed. Section 2 of *Blueprints: The Handwriting Book* gives alternatives for each of these letters so that most personal preferences can be accommodated.

Height of letters

This depends on the model chosen, or on your wishes if you are devising your own. It is usual for all ascenders to be the same height except for 't' which is usually a 'three-quarters' letter. Consideration must be given to the relationship of ascenders and descenders to minims; thirds gives a pleasing balance. Care must be taken to see that ascenders are not exaggerated.

Exit and/or entry strokes

Again, there are differing opinions about whether either or both of these strokes should be taught and how it should be done. If exit strokes are written more as a flick than a deliberate curve, the transition from cursive script to joining will be virtually spontaneous as children will begin to join letters almost automatically. Once this happens these families of diagonal joins should be taught followed by those with horizontal joins. Section 4 covers this stage of writing development.

Teaching entry strokes assumes that all letters join in the same way. This is not so. Think of letters in the same family as 'n' for example: when preceded by 'i' a different join is required from that if the letter is preceded by 'o'. Diagonal and horizontal joins attach themselves to letters in different ways. This can lead to awkward joins and misconstructions, sometimes making it look as though another letter has been inserted in the word. If only exit strokes are used in the beginning very little re-learning has to take place when joining is taught.

Ligatures
Do you want to teach joined writing from school entry? Or do you want a steady build up of skills before teaching exit strokes preparatory to joining? Or do you want joining to develop almost automatically from the style of writing taught? Teaching joined writing from the beginning, I believe, is asking children to cope with too much at once. Children need sufficient training in the movements which form letters and need to be taught exit strokes before beginning to join. They need to understand the individual character of the letters which make up our alphabet. If you teach letter shapes which lead naturally to joining some children will be joining letters by the end of their first year.

Learning to join is not difficult, it is a question of knowing what to do. Diagonal ligatures are not difficult to adopt because the exit stroke, in most cases, merely extends to make the join. Horizontal ligatures have a slight curve and need to be taught. Both diagonal and horizontal ligatures are taught in Section 4.

Specific letter changes when joining
There are a number of strongly held views as to whether the shape of any letters should change on joining. In most writing styles letters such as 'r', 's', 'x' and 'z' are changed when joining is introduced. Alternative forms for these letters are covered in Section 4 but the development work in Section 5 selects the letter forms which are fastest to write, which join easily and which have the most fluid movements. Some of us may find the shapes different from our practised hand but the letter shapes used are smooth and flowing, easy for children to adopt and control and will provide a firm basis for the development of a mature writing style.

Letters with no ligatures
Generally speaking the following letters are not joined: 'g', 'j' and 'y'. Opinion is divided about the shape of 'b', 'f', 'p', 'q', 's', 'x' and 'z' when joining and this affects the way in which they are joined. The more letters which can be joined the faster and more flowing the hand, consequently *Blueprints: The Handwriting Book* teaches children to join all letters except 'g', 'j' and 'y' in the best way possible for speed and legibility.

Terminology
The use of precise names should be consistent throughout the school. These are some of the terms you should consider and name.

1. The specific names to give different kinds of letters: upper and lower case, capitals and small letters or, and this is my preference, capitals and lower case. To call non-capitals small letters seems a misnomer because some letters are as tall as their capital counterparts.

2. The specific names to give parts of letters: stick, arch, ball, tunnel, flick, ascenders, descenders, minims, and their definition.

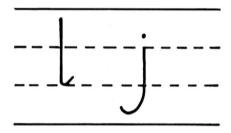

3. The language to describe different movements: up and round, down and round, clockwise, anticlockwise, forward, back, towards, away from, straight up and straight down.

Acceptable writing in different situations
Is it necessary or desirable for children to write to the best of their ability all the time? Opinions differ on this point. It would seem to make sense that, while they are learning the basic movements, children should copy the letters to the best of their ability. Once they are in control then, like adults, they should be free to adapt their writing as is relevant to its purpose, but at all times their writing should be both clear and legible.

The most important element is the correct movements that are made to form letters and in the onward movement to join them together because, once learned, these movements are never forgotten. When children know how to write they begin writing in a faster, more relaxed manner and the elements we have stressed from the start begin to come naturally. Once this happens time can be taken to concentrate on the look of the writing but if the focus on neatness is too strong, too early, incorrect movements may creep in which are difficult to correct later on.

THE THREE Ps

Posture

It is important to teach the correct posture for writing from the beginning and to build in strategies for remembering it until children automatically assume a good writing position. Ways of doing this include asking children to draw pictures of poor postural positions and good ones, making up songs, rhymes, mimes and plays with lots of talk and follow-up discussion to help reinforce and remind children of the importance of good posture for writing.

The way children sit at desks and the height of both the table and chair have an important part to play in how children write. If children cannot sit comfortably at their table they contort their bodies to achieve some element of comfort or at least to reduce the pain of an uncomfortable position. Different sized chairs and tables should be provided in each classroom so that the one best suited to each child is available. It may sound like pie in the sky in this day and age but some judicious exchanges between classrooms can help. If chairs and tables of different height are different colours it becomes easier for a child to recognise his or her 'own' table without the attachment of any stigma, but if you are stuck with what you have place a band of sticky tape or paint the top of the legs of matching tables and chairs with bands of the same colour so that they can easily be identified.

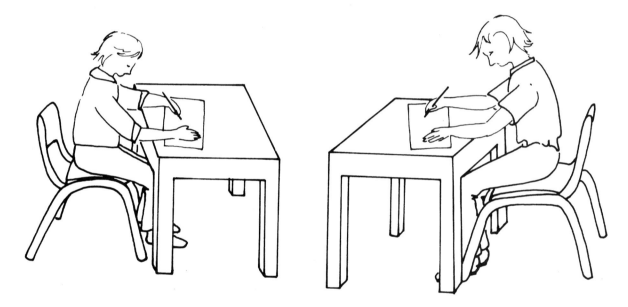

Good posture and a suitable sized table and chair are important.

Children need room to write. If their tables become too cluttered, or they are too crowded, children assume bad postural positions. Train them to put away (or place in a tidy pile) any items not needed for the task in hand and work on as clear a table as possible. This is a good habit to get into whatever piece of work they may be doing.

The relationship of the chair to the table affects writing. If the chair is too far away children bend at the lower back and sprawl forward in a half-lying position. Children who sprawl do not have the necessary control over their pencil and paper so poor letter formations creep in. Children should sit well back in their chairs with their feet flat on the ground and have sufficient leg room between the chair and the underside of the table. If the body is so close to the table that the stomach is touching it the free movements required for writing cannot be made. The optimum position is about a hand's width from the table so that the writer can lean slightly forwards, with a straight back, and have the whole of the forearm of the writing hand, not merely the wrist, resting on the flat surface of the table without needing to hunch the back or round the shoulders. The arm should be neither stretched nor cramped. Short people habitually have to sit at tables too high for them at school. Because of the years spent lifting their 'writing' shoulder as well as their writing arm in order to work more comfortably on the desk, and having to stick their head forward to read what was on the desk, they develop severe neck and shoulder problems later in life. Taller people have the opposite problem of sitting at tables too low for them, they hunch over their work, become round-shouldered and develop other kinds of back problems. Good posture for writing needs to become internalised so that it is automatically assumed whenever a person sits down to write. This will only happen if posture is taught correctly in the early years.

SUITABLE FURNITURE AT PRIMARY LEVEL

Height of table	Height of chair	Approximate age of pupils
550 mm	320 mm	5–7 years
600 mm	355 mm	7–9 years
650 mm	390 mm	9–11 years

As teachers we are not always aware of the problems strong sunlight or reflection may be causing our pupils. Check that there is no reflection from a work card, the paper being used, the chalk board and that children are not sitting in their own light. Some children hunch over their tables and hide their writing behind their hands, giving them extremely poor postures and obscuring the light. Such children need help regarding their posture but also confidence in what they do so that they feel no need to hide their work from their peers – or you! Light should come from the left for right-handers and from the right for left-handers whatever work they are doing. In crowded classrooms this is not easy to achieve but often just a slight change of position or exchanging place can achieve the required result.

Pens and pencils
Decide what restrictions, if any, you are going to place upon the writing implements children use and at what age. Traditionally, small children have been given fat pencils because they are said not to have the fine control needed for thinner pencils but most children will have been using normal sized pencils or ball-points at home long before they come to school so the argument is not as valid as was supposed. In any case fat pencils and crayons prevent tiny hands from using the correct grip and so allow bad habits to creep in. It is better to provide pencils of different thickness and shape: round, hexagonal, or triangular so that children can select the one with which they feel the most comfortable and which is best suited to their hands and their handwriting. Children should be encouraged to experiment with different implements. Even if they return to their original choice for general use, they will be able to choose confidently from a wider selection when the occasion demands or their needs change.

What about pens and when should they be introduced? Cartridge fountain pens or traditional steel dip pens? Fibre-tipped that do not smudge? What do you think about the use of ball-points? These are all decisions the school has to make but the more open a policy the school has on such matters the more it is to the advantage of the pupils who know the implement with which they feel the most comfortable at any one time. Fibre-tips slide smoothly over the paper, most children find them easier to use than pencils and so are ideal for exercises and remediation work.

Grip
Some children develop weird and wonderful ways of holding a writing tool even if they have no physical

problems, generally because of the way they first used a pencil at pre-school age. Also tension and anxiety may cause the child to hold a pencil too tightly causing muscle tension and so bringing undue pressure on the writing implement preventing an easy flowing hand. The writing implement should be held between the thumb and middle finger with the index finger resting lightly on the top forming a triangular grip. If the child has real difficulty developing this grip use a triangular pencil or buy triangular grips which fit over normal pencils and guide children's hands to learn the correct holding position.

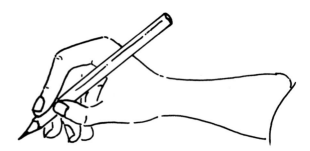

Thumb, middle finger and index finger should form a triangular grip.

Paper
In order to write properly children have to be able to see what they are doing so if the paper is not placed correctly they contort themselves into positions which become difficult to change. Right-handers should have their paper to the right of their body's mid-line and left-handers on the left (see illustration opposite). Incidentally, if these children sit together their writing arms should be on the outside and their papers looking towards each other so they are not in each other's way.

Young children need small sheets of paper because they have not yet learned to move their paper up to maintain a good writing position. With smaller sheets they do not have to reach so far when they write nor is the finished product on a piece of paper criss-crossed with folds where it has been bent over the edge of the table. In *Blueprints: The Handwriting Book* you will notice that the pages have been printed landscape and, in most cases, designed so that activities fit into sections of the page rather than the page as a whole. The line copymasters in Section 8 are designed to fit smaller pieces of paper.

The paper used should have a surface that causes the least possible tension yet not be so shiny and smooth that only faint images can be made with normal HB pencils or that fibre or ink pens slip on the surface and the ink, not being readily absorbed, is easily smudged. Paper is easier to write on if a few sheets of scrap paper, an exercise book or a colour magazine are positioned between it and the hard-topped table.

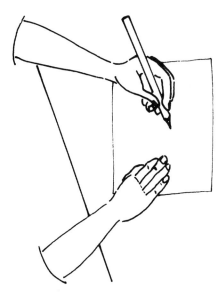
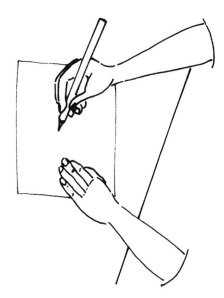

The paper should be to the left for left-handers and to the right for right-handers.

MOTOR CONTROL AND MEMORY

The place and use of lines

For more than four centuries the argument has raged between the use of lines versus blank paper and still today very firm opinions are held on the subject. Schools vary from those using unlined paper to those using paper with four lines on it, from those using a range of line spacing in all classes to those where all children use exactly the same size lines irrespective of their writing competence. In my opinion whether or not to use lines is dependent on the task and the competence of the writer. For instance many patterns and exercises need the freedom of blank paper while others benefit from lines. Presentation and writing for display looks better on unlined paper but most children find it difficult to write without lines.

Using a baseline helps beginner writers to give due consideration to the height differentials of letters and prevents their lines of writing running into each other. Paper with training lines and those with 15 mm gap between lines are best for beginners but once children gain control over their handwriting narrower lines should be available to them. As children's writing gets smaller, usually around seven, the space between lines needs to lessen but at primary level the minimum gap between lines should be 8 mm, closer than that encourages children to write too small and so develop a minute, cramped hand which is not what we are trying to encourage. If they are still made to use 15 mm spaced lines after their writing has naturally decreased in size, and are required to make all ascenders touch the line above, the resultant writing is too stretched and out of proportion. Continentals use books with small, lightly squared feints which impose neither size nor slant on the writer. Experiments in this country have shown that using books made out of squared paper has been helpful

in some cases. You may like to experiment with these with children who are experiencing difficulties in their control of the medium.

Children learning to write letter shapes and joins are helped by having training lines, which is why these are used in this book. Training lines help children to align their letters and understand the height differentials between letters. Children who have physical problems find that a baseline helps their orientation. It gives them a place from which to start, it also helps them to orientate their writing rather than be scared of a blank sheet of paper which has no reference point nor indication where to start. The temptation then is to say 'I can't' and scribble all over the paper in frustration.

Many children like to present their work on blank paper so that they can illustrate it but need guidelines under the paper to keep their writing straight. In Section 8 you will find a range of copymasters with different line spacing for children to use either under blank paper or to write on as necessary. These sets of lines make it possible for each child to have a photocopy of the lines best suited to their writing. It also means that you can use the same blank books in the class for all the children which apart from making life easier prevents differentiation between children and possible stigma.

Co-ordination

Children assimilate information in a range of different ways. These must be taken into account when teaching handwriting. Some children need a kinaesthetic approach, a sense of body position and movement, what the Greeks called 'muscle sense'. A few may be only able to learn from mnemonics, from an oral description of the movements involved to form a letter, whilst many learn visually.

11

Blueprints: The Handwriting Book combines all these approaches. Children look at the letters and the way they join (visual), they practise the movements which make the letter or join (kinaesthetic) and talk themselves through the movements using either the mnemonic given or devising one more suited to their style.

Handwriting skills require sophisticated eye-hand relationships and control over the fine motor muscles of arm, hand and finger. It also requires a degree of physical and intellectual maturity for the level of co-ordination necessary to form strokes correctly.

Despite the fact that handwriting is closely allied to both reading and writing, a child's reading or composing skills bear little or no relation to their ability to write a good clear hand. In fact handwriting can be mastered quite quickly by children who find reading difficult. Frequently it evades the grasp of children who are quick thinkers and good readers – perhaps because they learn quickly and are in too much of a hurry to put down their ideas to learn the repetitive skills of handwriting. But handwriting is a craft which has to be learned if a child is to be able to use this powerful form of communication to its best advantage.

Visual memory

Retention and recall are essential elements of learning. Visual memory involves the storing and being able to recall visual and perceptual experiences and, for most people, this is the way in which pictures, patterns, maps, directions and diagrams are remembered. By focusing on relevant details of stimuli giving increasing visual and verbal attention to them knowledge is stored in memory to use when the movement has to be performed.

Ways to help develop visual memory include the following:

●   showing children a letter or shape for a few seconds then asking them to find a matching one on a card or around the room
●   showing children a shape drawn on a card for a few seconds, then asking them to draw it from memory
●   Kim's game – noticing which items have been moved, removed or replaced from a collection involves storing and recalling visual information
●   reproducing simple shapes and diagrams from memory
●   colouring in a picture or pattern from memory
●   reproducing a sequence of colours from remembered instructions
●   completing drawings of well-known objects
●   matching pictures
●   putting pictures in order to show a sequence or tell a story
●   completing jigsaw puzzles
●   playing games like 'Snap' and 'Happy Families'.

Visual tracking

Tracking activities help children to follow movements with their eyes and to discern passage, action and movement. These activities include tracking the route from kittens through a tangle of thread to balls of wool, leading a dog to a bone, tracing a passage through a maze with the eyes before drawing in the route; drawing a pathway or route from spoken instructions using a photocopy of a simple map on which children trace a path with eye, with finger and then with crayons from one given point to another depending on the instructions given.

LEFT-HANDERS

If strategies for the needs of left-handers are clearly written into the school's policy document then fewer problems are likely to occur for these pupils. Points to consider are how the paper should be placed, which implement should be used, how it should be held, whether left-handers should be encouraged to have their wrist below or above the line of writing, the movements for specific letter shapes, who they should sit next to, how the light falls on their work and so on.

Teachers should learn to demonstrate with either hand, no matter which is their preferred one, then, although the writing by their less favoured hand may not be as neat as usual at least they will know what difficulties there are for children who write with the opposite hand and be able to help them. I found that, with a little practice, an acceptable level of writing was reached to enable this right-hander to help her left-handers.

The paper should be placed to the left of the body's mid-line and slightly slanted to suit individual needs so that the writing hand can move below the line without obscuring or smudging what has already been written. Left-handers should lean slightly forward over the table with the forearm resting on the table's surface and be positioned so that their elbow movements do not impede those of their neighbours, for example, sitting on the left of a double table. The chair should be high enough to enable the child to see over the writing hand and the light source should be from such an angle that the hand does not cast a shadow.

It may be helpful to fasten the paper to the table with masking tape in the very early stages but this should be dispensed with as soon as children are writing more than two lines. Children need to learn to move their paper with their non-writing hand while working in the way that right-handers do.

A suitable position for a left-hander.

The ideal implements are fibre-tipped pens because they are less likely to smudge than other implements. Be warned that too soft a pencil will smudge and too hard a one will dig into the paper. The writing implement needs to be held a little further back from the point than for a right-hander and a little more upright. The wrist should be below the line of writing with the end of the pencil pointing towards the child's left shoulder. Left-handers may feel a loss of control initially but if the fingers are lightly curled under the palm a stable base is formed sufficient to counteract any such feeling once they become used to the position.

The hardest things for left-handers are writing from left to right and making anti-clockwise movements. They will require a great deal of practice before the same level of proficiency is obtained as that of a right-hander. After the child has worked the first few activities in Section 1 reduce the size on the photocopier and let them repeat the task to encourage a greater degree of control.

Left-handers find it easier to write letters in the 'o' family in a clockwise direction (try it yourself and see why) so it is important to repeat the activities given for anticlockwise movements and find as many more as you can to strengthen this movement. Whilst the problem may not seem serious at single letter stage it becomes serious when joining commences because these incorrect movements make it impossible to join some letters.

Left-handers need to be watched closely because early detection and remedial treatment are essential if these children are to acquire a good hand.

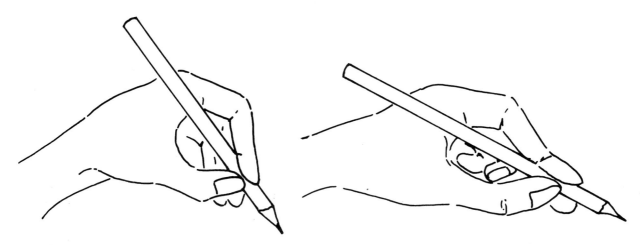

Wrist should be below the line of writing.

PRACTICAL ASPECTS OF TEACHING HANDWRITING

Handwriting can only be done with a child's willing co-operation so it is important that the way we teach it is one with which they feel comfortable and has activities they will enjoy. Young children should be told why it is important to use particular movements when forming a letter, older pupils should be told that they can improve their handwriting and eradicate bad practices if they are prepared to exercise sufficiently to replace old movement habits with new ones.

A good maxim for all teachers, irrespective of the age of the pupils or the subject is to teach systematically and imaginatively but to give enough priority to skills training for the children to obtain maximum gain from the subject. This is especially true of handwriting. We know that both good and bad habits are learned early, as are attitudes and behaviours, so we need to be sure that our attitude to handwriting and the way we teach it helps children to learn to write speedily, fluently and confidently. The way we teach handwriting must lead automatically from one stage to the next without giving rise to problems which could hold children back at a later stage.

It is the school which sets the model and the teachers who set the standard for their own classes. Frequently it is the teacher's own personal handwriting style which influences the work of their pupils hence it important that all the teacher's writing which pupils might see or read should be in the school's preferred style. Be a good model of that handwriting. Write in front of the children so that they can see how you write. Talk about what you are doing, how you are shaping the letters and what you need to think about. Draw attention to the letter's shape, talk through a mnemonic for the shape, discuss the kind of join and why. Provide plenty of examples of good handwriting and make sure that your writing on the board, in displays, in children's books is the best example you can provide. If your writing is awful, practise daily at home and whenever you are required to write anything at all.

Children obtain very little benefit from copying under the teacher's writing, from a card or from the board unless they are carefully observed and supervised. While some children's work will be a poor effort because of transference which has been discussed elsewhere, others will make a neat and what looks to be accurate copy. But how will each letter have been formed? Without supervision who knows where the 'I', or any other letter for that matter, will start and finish? How will you know if you were not there to see the letters being formed?

The biggest problem is fitting everything into the day. The most benefit I found came from spending between five and ten minutes teaching handwriting at the beginning of each day. In a mixed class of Reception and Year 1 children they watched me writing the letter as large as possible on the board making big, sweeping, flowing movements. We would draw the letter in the air together, reaching up as high as we could. We talked through the letter's formation as we made the movements. With their eyes closed, children drew the letter on the table top, in the palm of their non-writing hand, in the palm of a neighbour's hand while I went among them watching what they were doing. Only then would they practise writing the letter in their books. I wrote a single letter on the board while they watched then they would write it in their books while I watched them. We did this a few times then they suggested words which began with the letter or had the letter in it and I would write and they copy as before. Often during the day they would draw the practise letter in the sand, on the chalk board, painting it and making it in plasticine and so on. We had a letter table which not only had a collection of items beginning with the letter but also a laminated sheet of card with the letter on it, similar to those in this and *Blueprints: The Phonics Book* so that they could trace the movements which formed the letter with the index finger of their writing hand. Year 2's started the day in a similar way. We learned to join letters this way. Later in the year we focused on letters and joins children found difficult. The cumulative benefit of these few minutes every day was soon evident and it was gained without the need to allocate too much valuable time to it.

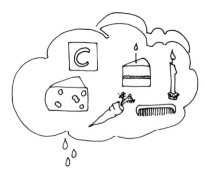

When teaching handwriting you need a clear model of the accepted school style and the progression from scribbling to fluent writing. *Blueprints: The Handwriting Book* provides a structured sequence for teaching handwriting. It begins with essential patterns and movements and follows with single letter formation, different ways of joining letters and practice material. At each stage children are reminded of how the strokes are made, how the letter or join is formed and where it starts and finishes. Your school will be following a similar structure and these copymasters should support what you are doing when you teach handwriting.

14

MAKING A START

Developing motor skills

Handwriting is, for the most part, a physical activity. It requires well-developed fine motor skills and good co-ordination if a child is to be successful in learning how to write quickly and legibly. Numerous activities taking place in the nursery and reception class help children to develop the motor skills needed for writing.

Activities which exercise control over larger muscles include:

- working with large and small apparatus
- ball activities
- skipping
- moving to music
- making music.

Activities which develop fine motor control and eye-to-hand co-ordination include:

- playing constructively with interlocking building bricks and other constructional toys
- modelling with clay and plasticine and papier mâché
- folding paper
- cutting along lines and around shapes using sharp scissors with rounded ends
- gluing and sticking shapes to form patterns and pictures
- making a picture from bits and pieces, drawing on chalk boards
- drawing in sand
- playing with tactile letters both bought and home-made from felt and sandpaper
- cutting out different ways of presenting single letters and pasting them on paper or card
- jigsaw puzzles
- tracing simple line drawings
- following pathways through mazes
- dot-to-dot pictures
- all forms of free drawing with crayons and felt pens
- tracing and copying patterns
- colouring in pictures
- drawing shapes and filling them in with patterns
- miming, action songs and rhymes.

Beginning

The pace of learning is different for each child. It is dependent upon the kind of home stimulus he or she has received. Parental interest and opportunities to draw, paint, look at books, roll dough into different shapes, shape it with cutters, use icing nozzles, kick a ball, wield a hammer and nails or use a screw driver all help the would-be writer.

Some children will have been taught to write at home and may come to school with incorrect pencil grips and faulty letter construction. They may hold a pen like a wooden spoon, write in capital letters, form letters from the bottom up or the wrong way round. If these faulty habits are not changed as soon as possible they will be set for a lifetime. From the moment a child enters school work should begin to identify any faults a child may have and to correct them straight away without stifling early attempts at emergent and creative writing. Teaching children how to form their letters correctly does not prevent emergent writing. It is more likely, in fact, to speed the development of a child's creative writing skills by giving them the tools with which to work.

Some children may have scarcely picked up a writing implement of any kind and have no idea how to form any letter. In some ways this group is easier to teach because they have formed no bad habits and can learn to do it correctly from the beginning but in other ways more difficult because they will need to go back to the beginnings, to nursery level, to scribble, to explore the marks that pencils and crayons make on paper and gain the sense of rhythm and flow needed for writing.

When children learn they need a balance between play, imitation, instruction and freedom to explore. When learning to write they need to trace over outlines, copy pictures and draw patterns as well as scribble, draw and create their own pictures and patterns. It is from their free work that you can judge the quality of children's pencil control and the amount of new learning that they are using.

Essential movements

The movements we want to encourage which are essential to good handwriting are left–right, top–down, anticlockwise, arching up and down, height and height differentials and correct spacing between letters and words. To do this children need good eye-hand co-ordination and pencil control.

Activities which encourage this include:

- drawing and painting recognisable figures – man, tree, house, toy
- free drawing
- drawing to spoken instructions – draw a straight line at the top of the page, draw a wavy line at the bottom of your page, draw a . . .
- feely bag, feel a shape in the bag with one's drawing hand, remove hand and draw the shape freely on paper
- draw or cut out a road and play cars on it
- make floor jigsaws in a group and draw it when completed
- copy patterns on pegboard from an example or copy from card
- cut out circles, squares etc. from magazines and make pictures with them
- trace simple shapes and pictures.

Teachers need to know which stage a child is at and what his or her needs are so as not to run counter to them. Watch children write as you move around the classroom so that you see how they form their letters and identify their specific weaknesses and strengths.

Writing corner

In the writing corner provide for both creative writing and handwriting so as to make the link from the letters they learn to write with those they use for writing down what they want to say. Put a choice of tables and chairs but identify which chair belongs to which table so as to prevent a mismatch. If your chairs and tables are not colour-matched and are the usual hotch-potch of finishes use self-adhesive sticky tape or paint a band of colour (tiny tins of paint for plastic models work quite well) near the top of each table and chair leg where it is less likely to get scuffed to identify which belongs with which.

Remember not to place your writing area in a dark corner, writers need good quality light coming from the correct angle but not so intense that it is too hot to sit there or makes light from the paper reflect into the eyes of the writer. Sometimes it is a good idea to have it by the windows in winter and away from direct sunlight in the summer.

Use a range of writing implements and different kinds of paper so that children can experience them and find out which suits them best. Their needs will change according to the task in hand. Have available pencils, pens, pencil grips, crayons, coloured pencils, paintbrush, felt pens, biros, fibre-tipped pens, ink, chalk, board, card, paper, sand tray, plasticine and a range of different papers. Posture, pencils and paper are discussed in more detail in 'The three Ps' on pages 9 and 10.

Patterns

Imitation and play have been important parts of a child's learning from birth, these combined with encouragement and good example from the teacher are essential to the development of a specific skill like handwriting. Remember that learning to write is a long slow process, if you try to hurry it the result will be less than satisfactory.

Once children have found the delight of scribbling, that when a writing instrument and paper come together and the hand moves the one over the other the result is magic, they are ready to progress along the pathway that leads to a form of expression, unique to Homo Sapiens, which can be both public and private. Not all children come to school with this experience and will need time to explore the medium.

Joined patterns should be taught alongside cursive letters to help children develop the flow, rhythm and consistency essential for writing a good hand. The following patterns are suitable for pre-school and nursery children and can be introduced soon after scribbling has begun. They are also suitable for others, children or adults, who need help with their writing. Early efforts may seem nothing like the desired result, but practice brings control which, in a year or two, brings the skills needed to perfect their attempts – provided that their teachers fully understand the patterns and purpose of the models they set before the children. The patterns illustrated below are those which are necessary in letter formation and in developing a relaxed, flowing handwriting style.

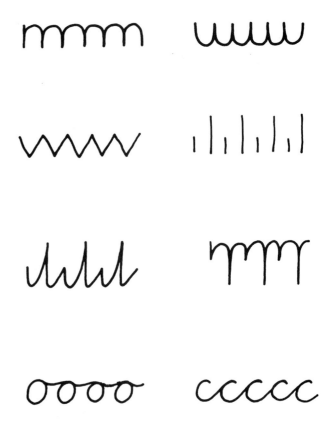

Children who practise rhythmic pattern movements from the beginning have a head start because there is much to learn. For example:

- which end of the instrument makes the marks on the paper
- how to hold it to get a result
- how strong a grip is needed
- how to keep the paper still while the instrument moves
- how to control the movement
- how to make the pattern
- how to transfer what they see on to their own piece of paper
- how to match its size, height and repeat it
- how to listen to and take in the adult's instructions
- the need to work from left to right.

After the initial excitement of making marks on large sheets of plain paper with thick and thin pencils, crayons and fibre-tipped pens in their first few weeks in school and they begin to write what they consider to be words, encourage children to reduce their patterns near the size of their normal handwriting because if the patterns they learn to form are to be transferable to that child's handwriting they must have relevance to it.

Most children need time to learn to copy the pattern correctly, some children may take as long as a year to get it right, but provided you, and they, know what is being aimed for you can encourage the children to work towards a good result. Be aware that some of the patterns recommended in other books do not help children to develop an easy, flowing style, rather they establish movements which work against the children developing a good hand.

16

Display

Display children's work whenever possible, if only for the day, so that they develop a sense of pride, achievement and self worth. Young children like to take their work home at the end of the day so if it is a piece of work you will want to keep or to put up again ask them to bring it back the next day or invite their parents in to see it in the display. Children's personal folders of work should be shared with their family. It is your decision whether they may be taken home overnight or the parents come in to

see them. In sharing their work children explain the nature of the task they have been doing and point out the growth points you will have talked about together.

Balancing needs of one-to-one and whole class teaching is no easy task but if you class teach handwriting for a few minutes at the beginning of every day and at other opportune moments it will take just a few seconds to deal with problems you observe during the rest of your classroom activities.

RECORDS OF ASSESSMENT ▶

What kind of records need to be kept?
Children should have a folder in which to keep samples of their handwriting. The work needs to be dated. Sometimes it is helpful for children to write their own comments on the reverse side stating what they think of that piece of writing. By looking back children can see the progress they have made, become their own arbiter and critic which, in turn, becomes a motivating element towards making even greater improvements.

Representative examples of work should be kept which show which writing was dictated, copied or freely written, everyday writing, writing for others and for display ('best' writing). Keep sample work from each term which highlights the child's progress or a problem area which needs to be resolved, note problems or any letters the child may be finding difficult and the remedial action you took. This will be beneficial to the teacher who will be responsible the following year. Another benefit will be that, after a few years, samples of work of children moving up through the school from reception will show how successful a model the school has chosen.

What to look for when assessing children's handwriting
Assessment is part of record keeping but it is also constructive in helping the pupil to move forward, whatever the subject being assessed. In handwriting, what kind of things is reasonable to assess? What is important is developing a good hand?

The main criteria for assessment must be:

- are the basic movements correct
- does the child start and finish letter movements in the right place
- are the height differentials correct
- does the writing flow, is it rhythmic
- are the words appropriately spaced
- is the writing legible
- is the grip correct
- is the angle of the paper and the child's posture satisfactory?

These criteria can be assessed by close observation of the child in the act of writing. Individual discussion can help children to understand what is important and to focus on these elements. This in turn helps their writing to improve.

DEALING WITH PROBLEMS ▶

Children with handwriting problems are much fewer than those with reading problems – in fact some of the least able children can learn to write well even if, sometimes, they are unable to read what they write. The correct movements must be taught from the start but if any errors are identified they must be remedied straight away if they are not to become ingrained.

In order to diagnose difficulties you need to make yourself familiar with the normal development of children's handwriting, know what to expect and the range within which a child should function at a certain age to know whether he or she is outside that parameter

and the extent to which he or she may be having problems.

If a child is experiencing problems you need to analyse what those problems are and set up a programme to remediate them. Items on your checklist when observing children should include letter formation, entry points, exit points, spacing between letters and between words, inadequate ascenders or descenders, the inappropriate use of capital letters. Any one of those points can mitigate against the development of a good handwriting style. It is worth taking time to talk these points through with children so that they are clear in their heads what they should be aiming for and why.

Some children do not develop a good hand because of inadequacies in the way they have been, or are being, taught. Children need to know what is to be aimed for and how to work towards it. Which are the most important rules for children to learn? There are just three of them, and armed with these both children and teachers can improve their handwriting within a matter of months.

1. Each letter has a correct starting and finishing point.
2. Letter heights must be consistent – ascenders should be the same height and sit on the line, minims consistent in height and sit on the line, descenders the height of minims but with their 'tail' below the line.
3. All down strokes, whether they be for ascenders, minims or descenders, must be parallel.

Dealing with difficulties and common problems

The majority of problems can be dealt with provided they are caught early enough. Usually they are only of a minor nature, poor performance rather more than significant difficulties. Observation will bring these to light and, with help, they can soon be corrected. The most important factor is a good teacher/pupil relationship. It has to be caring, concerned, but most of all patient. If children have handwriting problems then it is the teacher's job to take positive steps to help them, it is not something children can do by themselves.

If proper attention is paid to teaching the style of handwriting thoroughly at the beginning and potential problem areas worked through carefully and clearly then problems are much less likely to occur. At Junior level, if the children are given a short refresher course at the beginning of the year to remind them of what is expected, any specific problems can be dealt with on an individual or small group basis as they are noticed during the year.

Physical difficulties

Children with physical difficulties and those with poor motor control find unjoined writing easier because they need only focus on one letter at a time. They need to move slowly and master one letter or group of letters before moving on to the next. The same is necessary for children with mild spasticity.

Incorrect movements

There is no miracle cure for incorrect movement patterns only practice, activities, observation and hard work. A detailed explanation of each step in forming a letter shape is needed – even if it means going back to the earliest stage of pattern-making and letter-formation and then gradually leading the child forward again.

First of all children should practise the letter or its join by standing up and making big, huge, enormous letters moving across the body line. You should talk them through the actions while you make the letters together. Some teachers prefer to draw the letter in the air with their back to the children because they are then facing the same way as the children. My experience is that when you are facing the children you can see what they are doing and they can see clearly the movements you are making. Practice will make you a dab hand at drawing an image of any letter so that it is correct for the children but a mirror image for you. Through this activity children also learn to start and finish letters in the right place.

Face the children when you draw letters in the air so that they can see the complete letter shape.

18

Writing the problem letter themselves as big as they can on a chalk-board, painting it on large paper and making cross body writing movements, especially to music, all help children to reinforce the pattern prior to working from the copymasters. Writing in a tray of sand, using crayons on big sheets of paper, painting letter shapes, feeling sandpaper letters with start and stop places clearly identified, dipping a stick in a bucket of water and drawing letters on a hard outside ground surface, anything you can think of which helps reinforce the correct movement. But you must watch what the child is doing to make sure that letters begin and end in the right place and that the correct movement is formed.

Height differentials

Draw four lines on the board and highlight each of the three spaces with a pale colour then, in white chalk, write the letters of a word or family group firmly so that they stand out from the colours. If you are working on ascenders sorting out their height in relation to minims and the position and length of descenders you may wish to shade only the top or the middle space. You can emphasise ascenders and descenders in relation to minims (or the 'x' height as it is sometimes known) by highlighting either the middle or the outer spaces.

Spacing

Uneven spacing can be caused by tension or too much pressure causing the pencil to jerk. It can also be because a child does not have the concept of words as wholes. The use of exit strokes helps children to space letters correctly and if (at the beginning) we encourage children to leave the space of their little finger between words, words become defined as wholes. As soon as children have the concept of words as wholes and know the size of a letter 'o' suggest their using that as an alternative, spacing between words then becomes

related to the size of their own writing and they are less likely to write words with vast gaps between them.

Legibility

Problems here are often due to the child's thinking being faster than the pen can follow so destroying any semblance of good handwriting. Doesn't this happen to us too? If the child is really fired up with a story, tape it or ask a parent to write it at the child's dictation for the child to copy (if the work warrants it in the child's eyes) in their own time. This way handwriting is not sacrificed to inspiration and inspiration is allowed to flow at its own rate.

Visual perceptual

Children who exhibit visual perceptual difficulties have difficulty in recognising and differentiating letter shapes which is often revealed by such faults as mirror imaging or reversals. Children need to repeat the strokes which form a letter several times gradually putting them together until they have assimilated the movements and can form the letter without help. Only then should they begin to join that letter with another equally well-known one.

Reversals

Letter reversals are not uncommon until a child is about seven. With younger children it is not something to be unduly concerned about but advice should be sought if it continues. Children should practise the letters they reverse by making large letter shapes which cross over the body's mid-line. With letters like 'b' and 'd' it can be helpful for children to put their hands together with palms facing towards them, finger tips to finger tips as illustrated below.

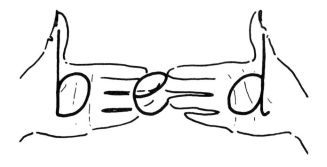

The best way is to solve this problem I have found is to teach a closed 'd' but an open 'b'. These two letter forms require different movements and look different so that confusion is eliminated. Some people recommend teaching words made from 'a' and 'd' such as 'add', 'dad' and 'dog' and 'bobby', 'bap' and 'pub' to remind children

of each letter's correct shape and sound but, quite honestly, the open 'b' solves the problem.

With other letters likely to become reversed, such as 'n' and 'u', discuss with the child the words that come to mind when they think of the letters and devise a word, symbol or amusing mnemonic to enable them to complete the letter strokes correctly. For example, for 'w' and 'm': the arches for 'w' have to be open at the top so that it can be filled with water, 'm' is the sticky-up ears of a mouse who hates water in his ears so the arches have to be closed by the line. It's nonsense, I know, but it sticks in children's minds and helps them to remember which way up to write the letters.

Cross laterality

Children with right hand/left foot dominance (or vice versa) may also experience similar difficulties. They need practice, persuasion, patience, perseverance and then more practice with lots and lots of activities such as matching shapes, tracing and dot-to-dot pictures and letters similar to those in Section 2.

Copying

Young children have difficulty in transferring letters and words from long sight (the blackboard) to near sight (their paper), and the younger the child the more difficult this task becomes. They lose the place they were copying from, copy words incorrectly and generally become totally confused. Such copying is of no real educational benefit for young children anyway even if they experience no real difficulty in so doing. Children need to work from material close at hand, either immediately beside or above the paper on which they are writing, where they can keep track of the place they have reached and easily identify the letter or word that comes next.

Even this may be too difficult for some children so prepare a piece of card with a narrow window in it which will expose only three or four words. The child moves it along, one word at a time, in such a way that he or she can see the word they are to write plus the one they have written and the one which comes next. This way they keep the word in the context of what they are writing. Another aid is a piece of acetate with an arrow on it which the child places over a word once it is written so that the arrow points towards the next letter to be written but the whole text can be seen clearly.

Knowing where to start

Some children find difficulty in writing from the left side of the page, particularly left-handers. Some children start on right, others write snake-like – line one left to right, line two right to left, others mirror image facing pages. Two ways of helping children are to place a green (for go) dot at the beginning of each line on the page until the children can do it for themselves remembering without an aid or to place a coloured strip along the edge of the page as a reminder of which end of the line to start writing. Another way is to draw a margin on each page so that a child's first letter is written touching it.

PART 2
THE
COPYMASTERS

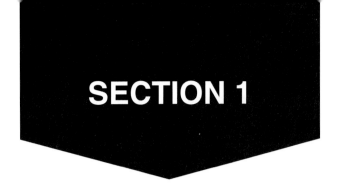

SECTION 1

MOTOR SKILLS

C1–18

In this section children begin by learning the left to right direction of our language then the strokes and movements used to form the basic letter shapes in written English. Children learn the precise nature of these strokes through rhythmic patterns. These help children to develop flowing movements and experience the essential nature of cursive writing before they have actually learnt to write.

Patterns are not just a way into writing, nor just a means of getting the hand and finger muscles ready for the specific movements required for writing. They are also useful for developing rhythm and flow and for exercise and correction throughout the development of a child's handwriting. Not all pattern work is helpful in developing a good hand, some lead to poor perception and work against the development of correct letter formations. Be very critical of the writing patterns you use with your class and avoid these ones:

 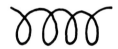

The pattern movements are worked in groups of five or six, in word lengths, so that they can be written without needing to move the hand during the pattern. This makes it easier for the child to copy and the stroke is less likely to deteriorate.

The order suggested is flexible once directionality has been established. If you see a child drawing a pattern in scribble or free work it makes sense to give them the copymaster which helps them to refine the one they are enjoying rather than sticking to the given order.

Copymasters 1–4
Use visual tracking to trace the pathways, first with the index finger of the writing hand then with left to right eye movements. Next children close their eyes and practise the pattern on the table top several times before drawing a line along the pathway with crayons. Children should draw the pathway on the copymaster repeatedly with different coloured thin crayons, felts or pencils, trying to become swifter and more direct each time to build up confidence.

The copymaster pages can be treated in a number of ways to aid visual tracking skills. Print or mount the photocopy on card then paint the pathway with PVA® glue; paint either side of the pathway with glue and sprinkle it with sand; paint either side of the pathway with Liquetex® (available from craft shops) using their sand, stucco or stone finishes; cut fabric to shape and glue either side of the pathway. All these treatments make the pathway smooth and the area surrounding it rougher to the touch so that the index finger of the writing hand can trace the stroke smoothly in the correct direction. These treatments work equally well for the letter shapes in Section 2.

Copymasters 5 and 6
The dotted lines should be drawn in with swift downward strokes; it is the movement more than a careful tracing over the lines that matters. These strokes prepare for the family group of 'i', 't', 'l', 'j', and the downward strokes on all minims and ascenders.

Copymaster 7
Joining the letters in the dot-to-dot patterns not only reinforces the alphabet but encourages children to make straight strokes in a number of different directions.

Copymaster 8
The children practise two directional strokes before combining them in preparation for 'x', 'z', the angular form of 'v', 'w', 'k' and 'y' plus most capital letters. They should practise the stroke by writing over the solid line, then use the dotted line as a guide before writing the stroke for themselves.

Copymaster 9
Children look for and fill in the parts of the drawing which are in dotted lines. It encourages them to look at parts of a shape rather than the whole so they become aware of how it is made up.

Copymasters 10–12
These copymasters practise the arching up strokes needed for the letter family of 'n', 'm', 'h', 'r', 'p', the cursive 'k' and the closed 'b', using firstly a broad arch then tighter ones more akin to the letter shape. The

return up stroke but must go over the down stroke not form a loop at the bottom.

Copymaster 13
Here the arching down stroke is practised for '**u**' and '**y**', the curved '**v**' and '**w**' and the open '**b**'.

Copymaster 14
The anticlockwise movement for letters '**c**', '**o**', '**a**', '**d**', '**d**', '**q**', '**e**', '**s**', '**f**' is introduced here as well as free flowing lines. Once learnt, children can draw balloons

and strings freehand with other media and surfaces to develop confident swift flowing movements.

Copymasters 15 and 16
The spirals on these two pages are to reinforce the anticlockwise movement so that the action becomes free and flowing.

Copymaster 17
All the strokes in this section are brought together in this picture. Children start on the solid line and follow the direction of the arrow to complete the stroke.

Copymaster 18
Mazes are ideal for visual tracking. First trace with the finger, the eye, then with a crayon as detailed for Copymasters 1–4.

Name _____

Name _____

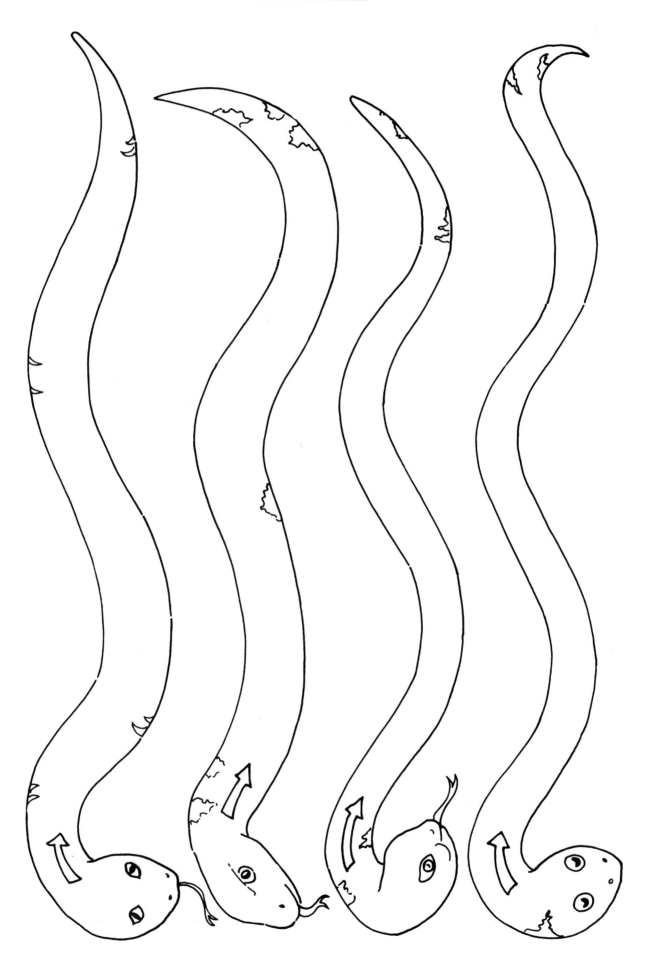

Name _____

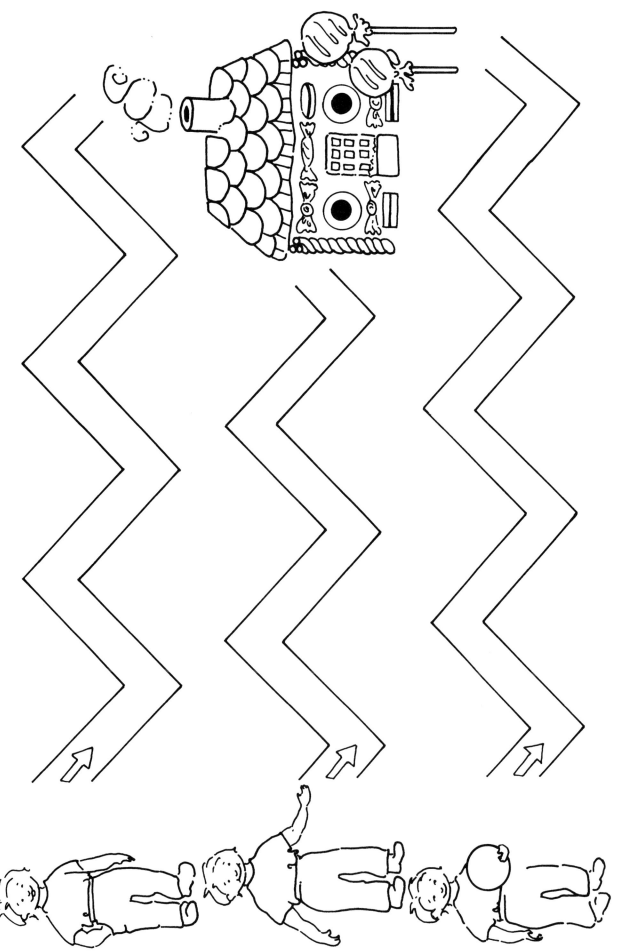

Name _____

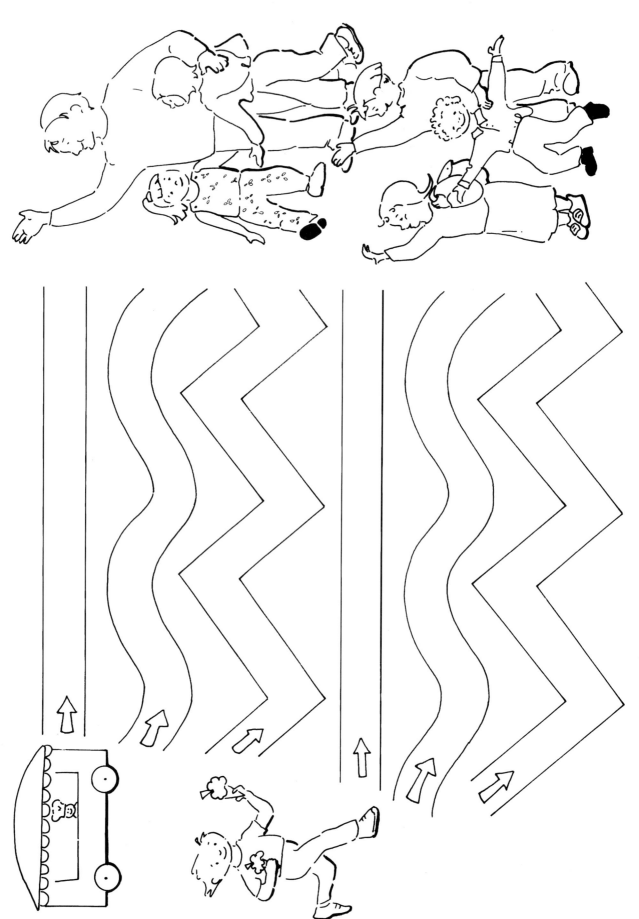

Name _____

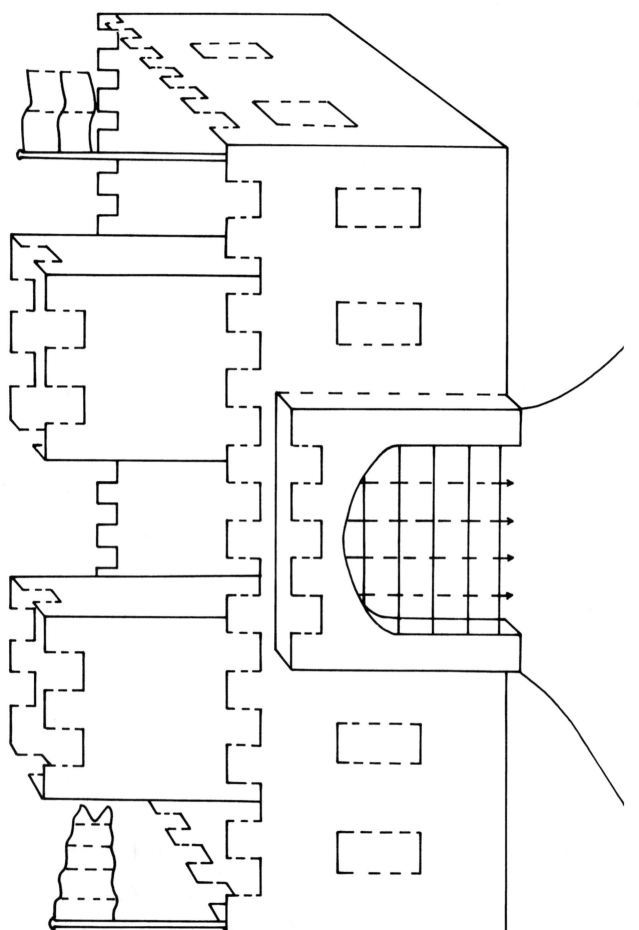

Copymaster 6

Name _____

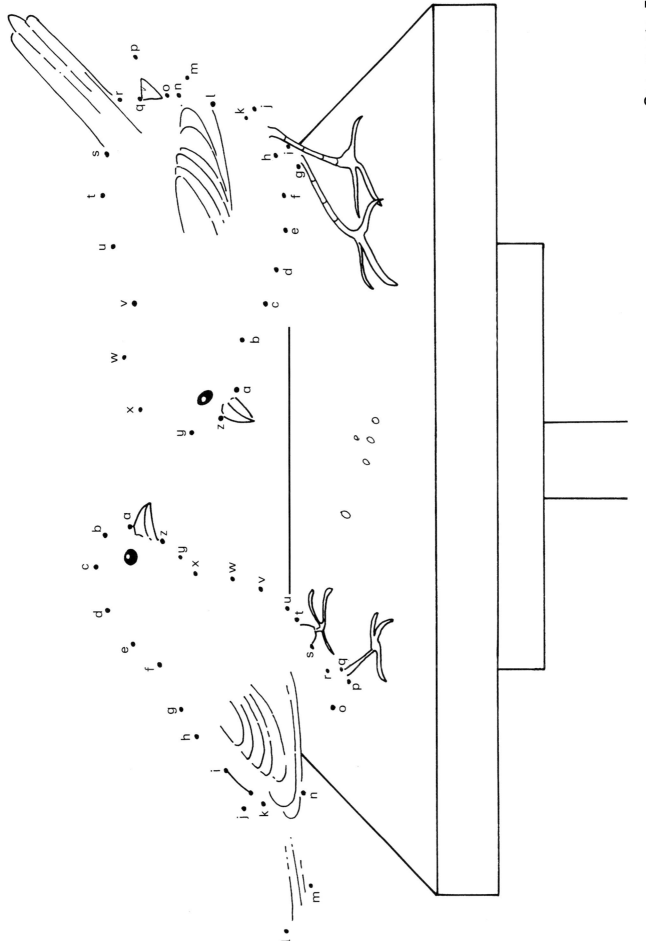

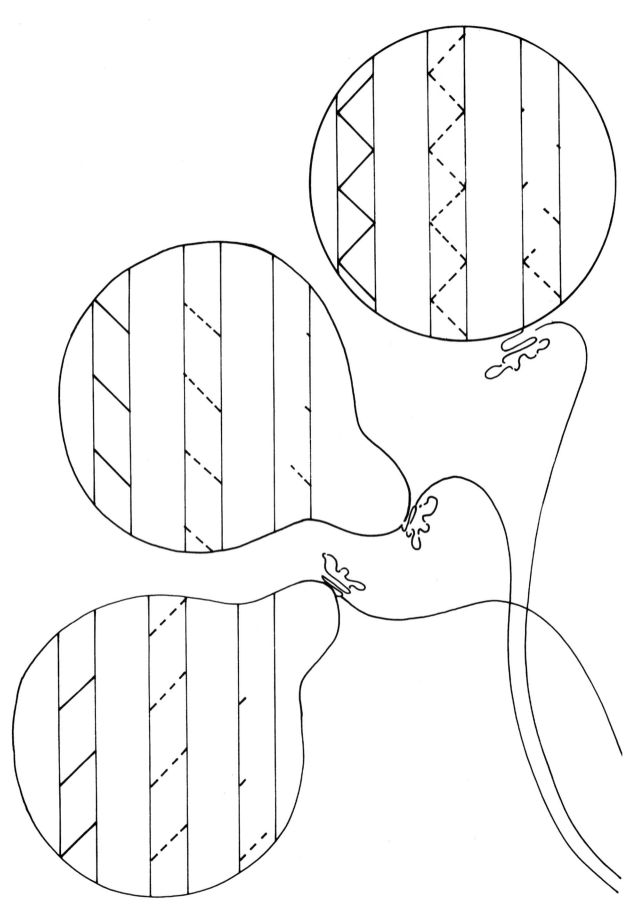

Name _____

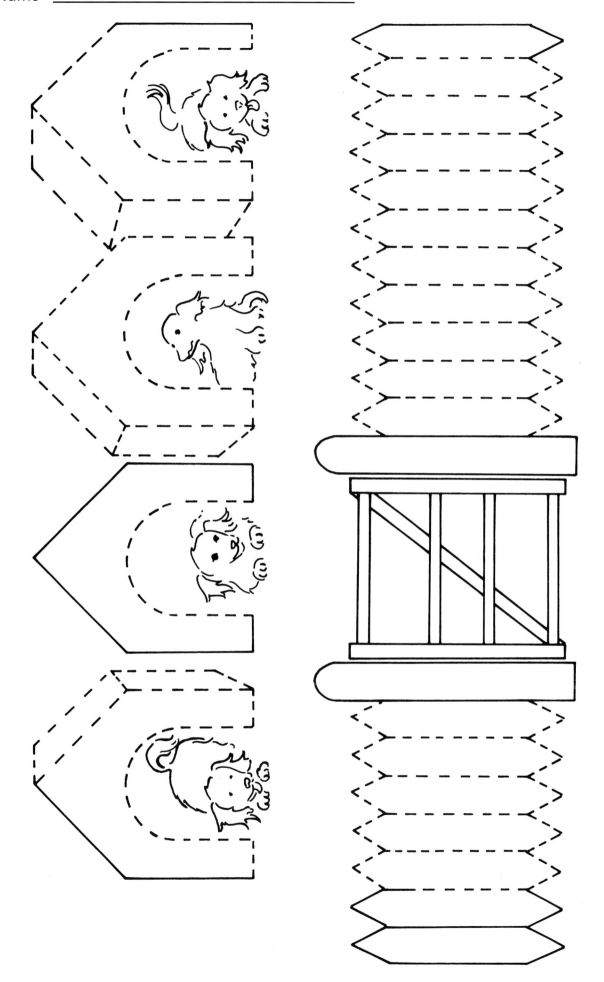

Name _____

Name _____

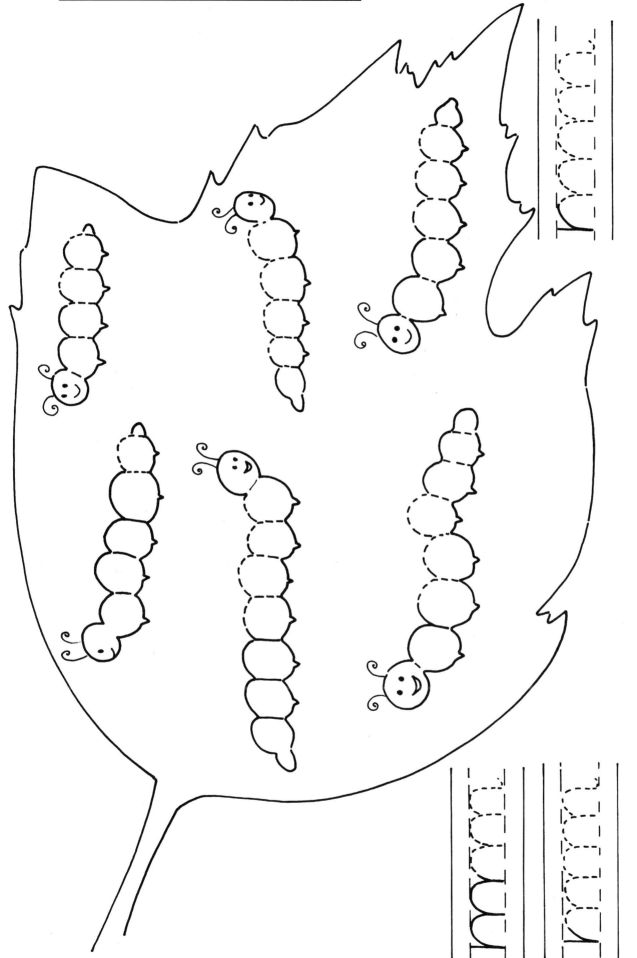

Name _____

Name _____

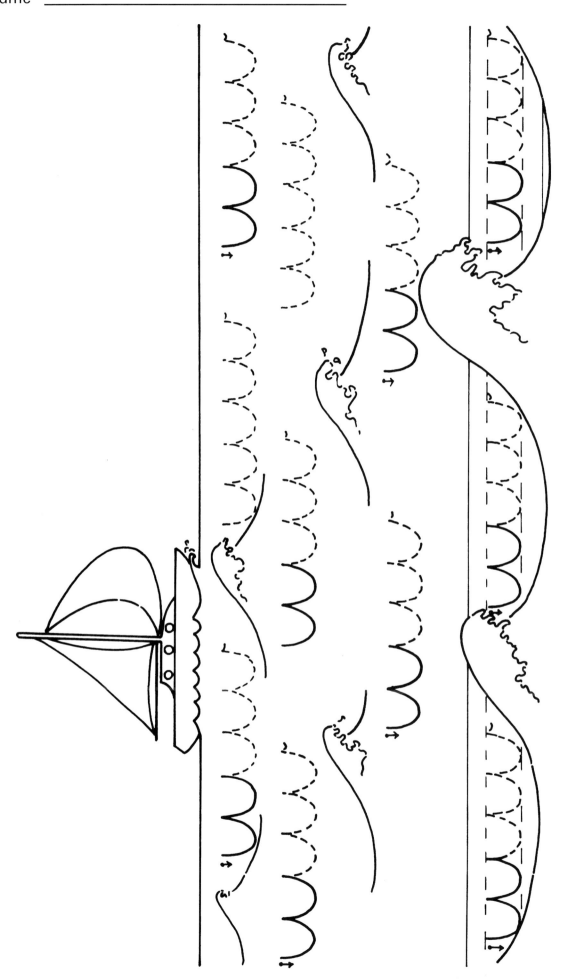

Name _____

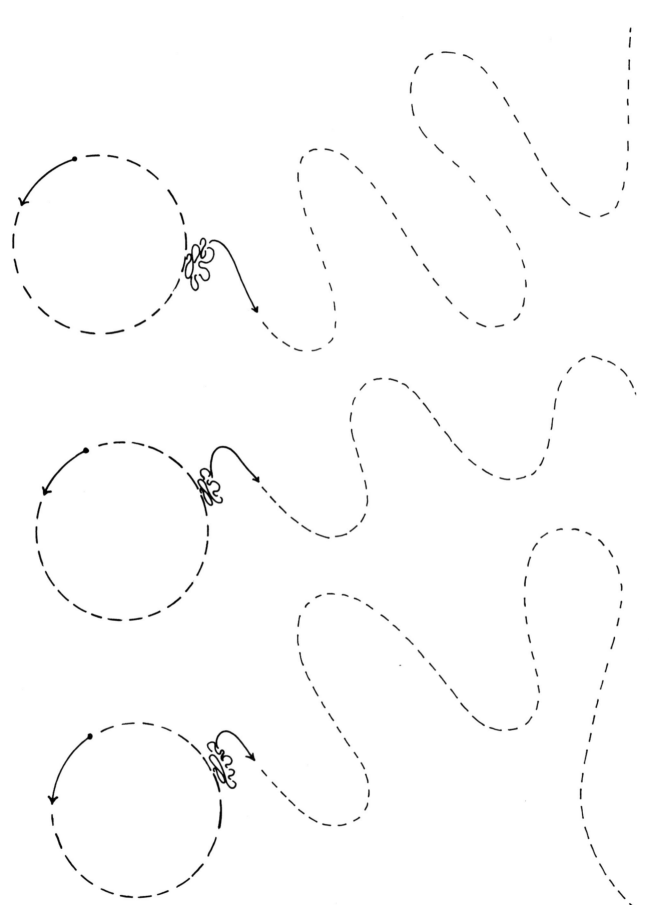

Name _____

Name _____

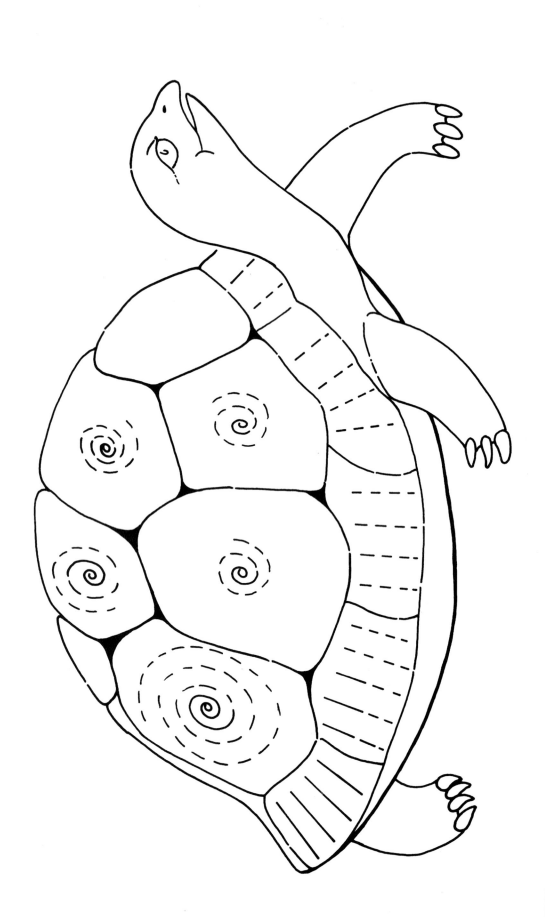

Name _____

Name _____

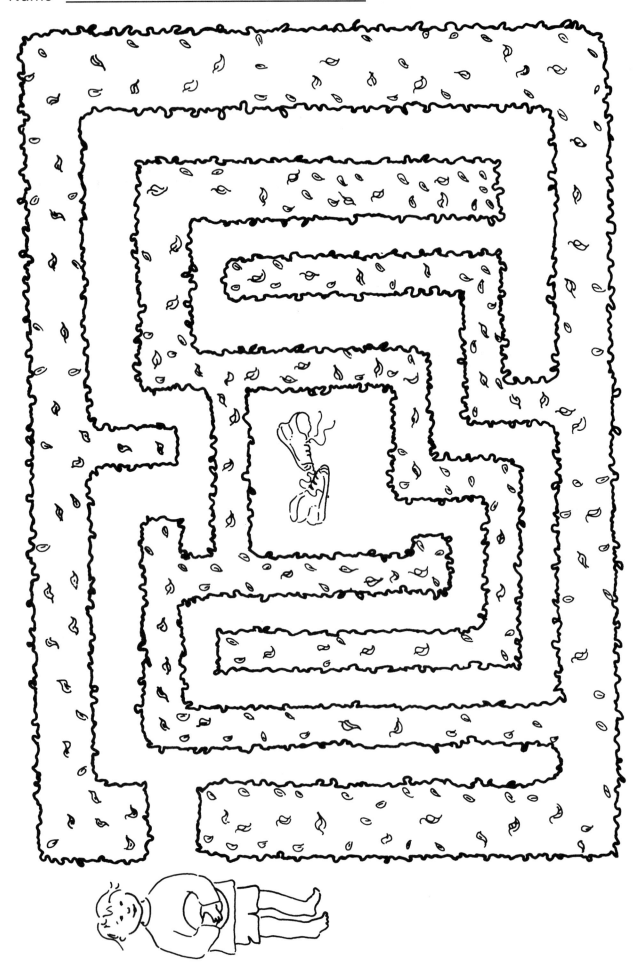

SINGLE LETTERS

In this section letters are taught in stroke related families rather than alphabetically. This helps children to learn a particular series of movements more quickly and to reinforce that learning. Children learn to write more quickly with this kind of built-in redundancy. Children should be told why it is important to execute particular movements when forming a letter.

When introducing a letter shape ask the children to stand up and draw the letter with you, in the air, from above their heads to the ground and right across the mid-body line. Let them sit down and write it on the table top with their writing finger, then with their eyes closed, then over the letter shape on the appropriate copymaster.

Make up mnemonics for writing letters shapes using appropriate language such as 'down the stick, up and round the tunnel and flick up' for 'h' or 'up and round, down and round, straight up, straight down and flick up' for 'd'. Some children find it more helpful if they make up their own. If the mnemonic for a letter shape has an inner rhythm it helps children to write rhythmically as they say them to themselves. It also stops them rushing through the letter until they are sure of its movements.

Letter patterns can be traced in the sand, drawn in chalk on a chalk board or on the playground, traced on the floor with a pointed toe, walked around patterns drawn in chalk on the floor. See Making a Start (page 15) for other suggestions for reinforcement.

Letter shapes should be made a number of ways:

● from rolled Plasticine® and the movements which form it traced with a pointed index finger
● tracing and tracking the letter shapes
● cutting them out of paper and filling them in with a series of correct letter strokes
● drawing them in sand, tracing them in sand with a stick
● drawing them with finger paints.

Letter families and associated patterns

The letters below have been grouped into families according to the nature of their stroke. Writing movements are reinforced when letters are practised together which are built on similar strokes.

Different alphabets have varying letter shapes so, where possible, the most common variants have been included. In the groups below, where letters have more than one construction and so belong to more than one group these letters have been placed in brackets.

Letter families	Patterns for practice
1. *i t l u j (b v w y)* **Copymasters 19–27**	*uuu uuu*
2. *n m r h p p (b* **Copymasters 28–35**	*mm mm*
3. *c o a d g q e s* *s f f* **Copymasters 36–45**	*cccc cccc*
4. *x z (k v w y)* **Copymasters 46–51**	*vvv vvvv*

Other useful patterns include:

c c c c with its forward and back movement is a difficult one to learn but perseverance is important because one of the largest families of letters depends on this formation.

Copymasters 19–51

This group of copymasters follow the order in the table above.

On the copymasters all letter strokes start with a dot and forward pointing arrow. It may help some children to have this dot coloured green (for go). All strokes stop at the cross. This could be marked red (for stop).Where two separate strokes form the letter the dots and crosses are marked 1 and 2 respectively. Rounded letter shapes have been used to ensure clear formation. As a child's handwriting matures the shapes will become more oval, like the handwriting of most adults. Generally there is an association between the letter being practised and the picture to reinforce its name or sound.

43

- Before the children start work talk about the strokes which make the letter. Ask them to draw it in the air, on the table, on the palm of their non-writing hand or on a neighbour's hand.
- Children should trace the letter between the outlines first with their fingers then with pencils, crayons or felt pens.
- They trace over the dotted letters on the lines then write them by themselves. The letters are practised on training lines to help children develop a sense of its shape and position in relation to other letters. The space between the solid lines is divided into three by dotted lines for this purpose. The 'x' height of each letter, the main part, is written between the dotted lines. The ascenders and descenders are written within the spaces above and below.
- The picture includes the dotted letter shape for children to write over as often as possible for further practice and to encourage letter association.
- The picture can be coloured in as this helps to develop children's control of a writing or drawing implement.

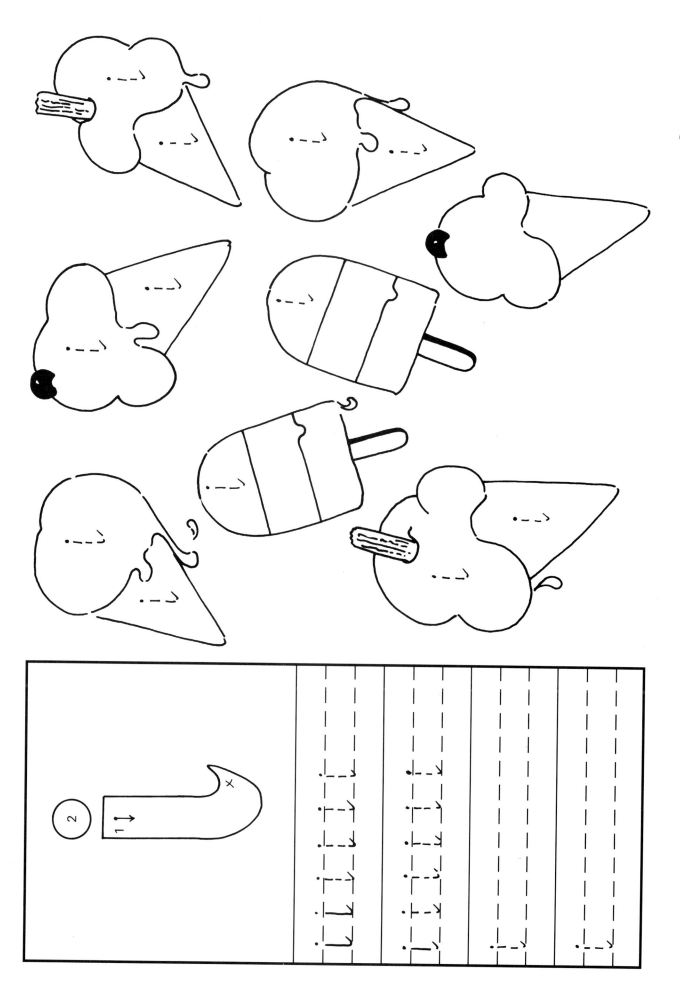

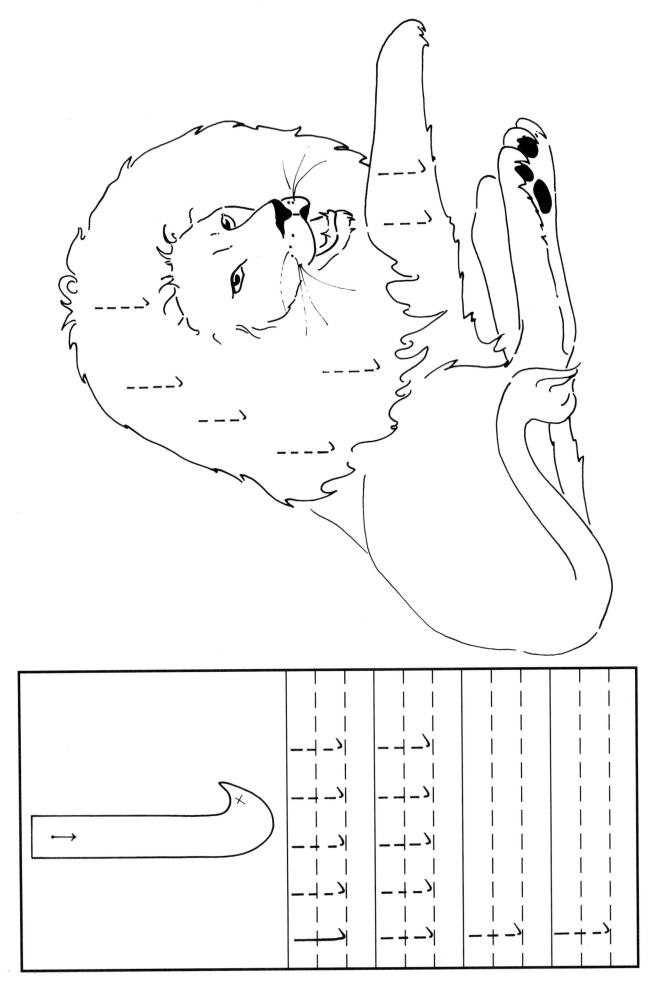

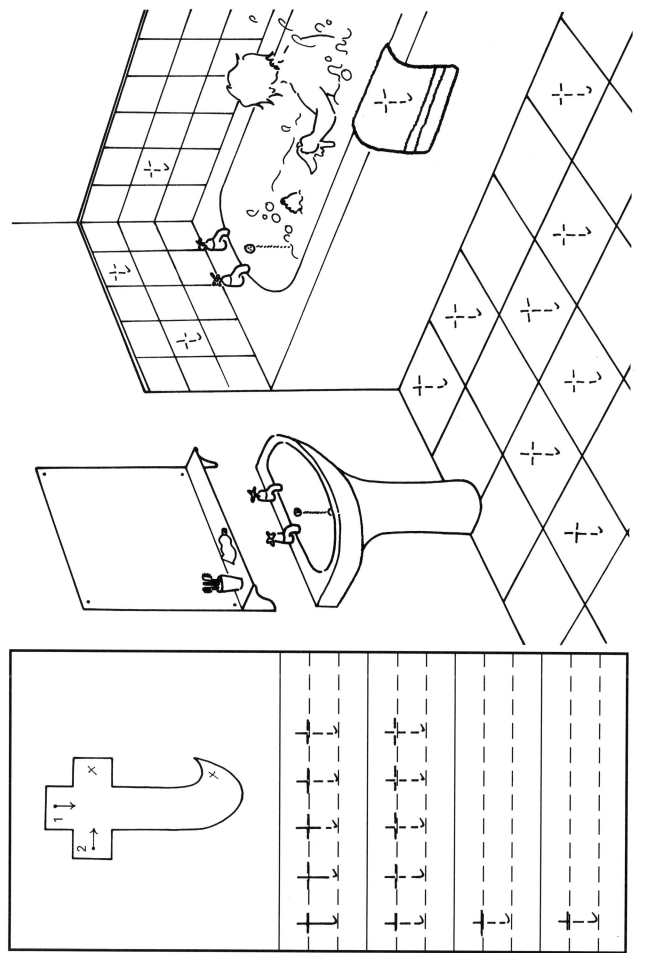

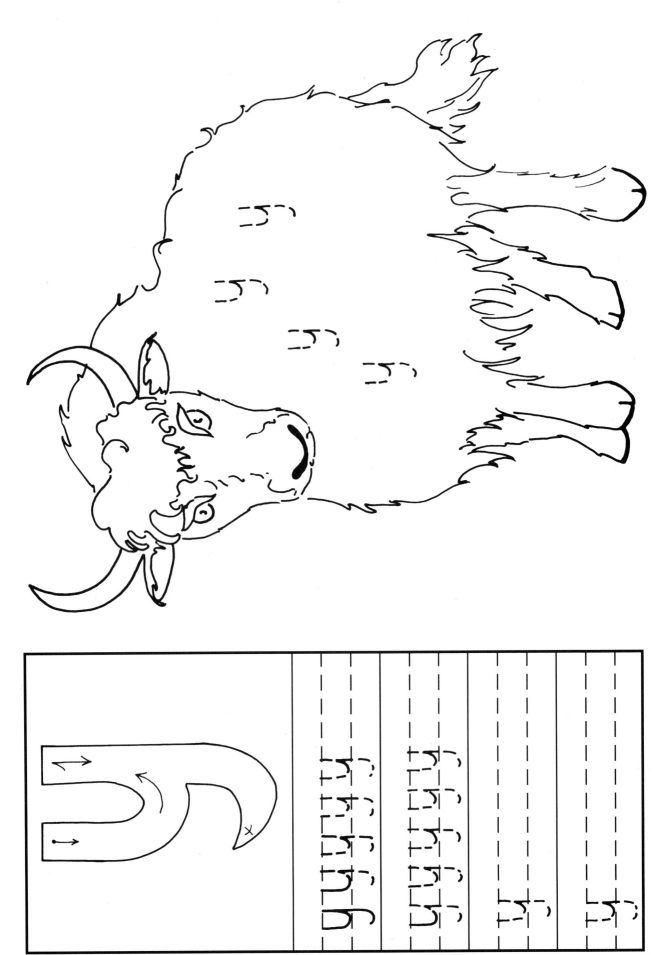

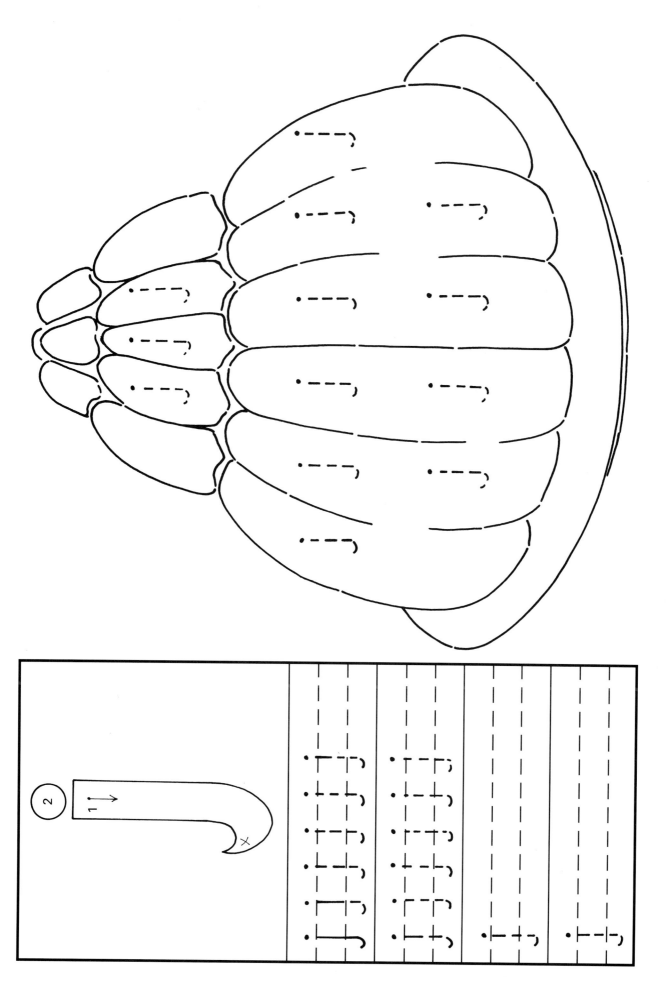

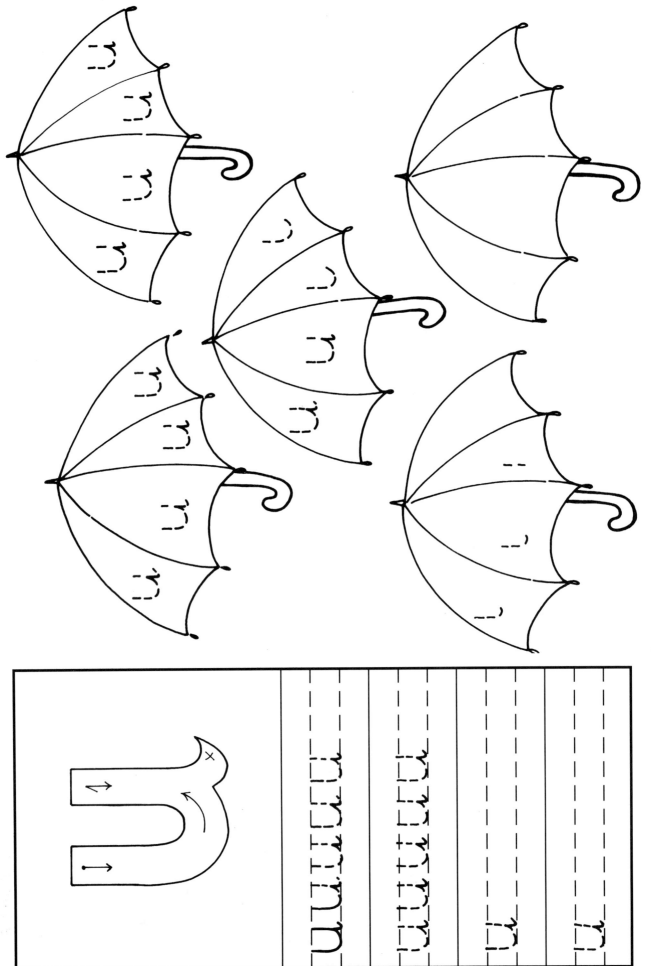

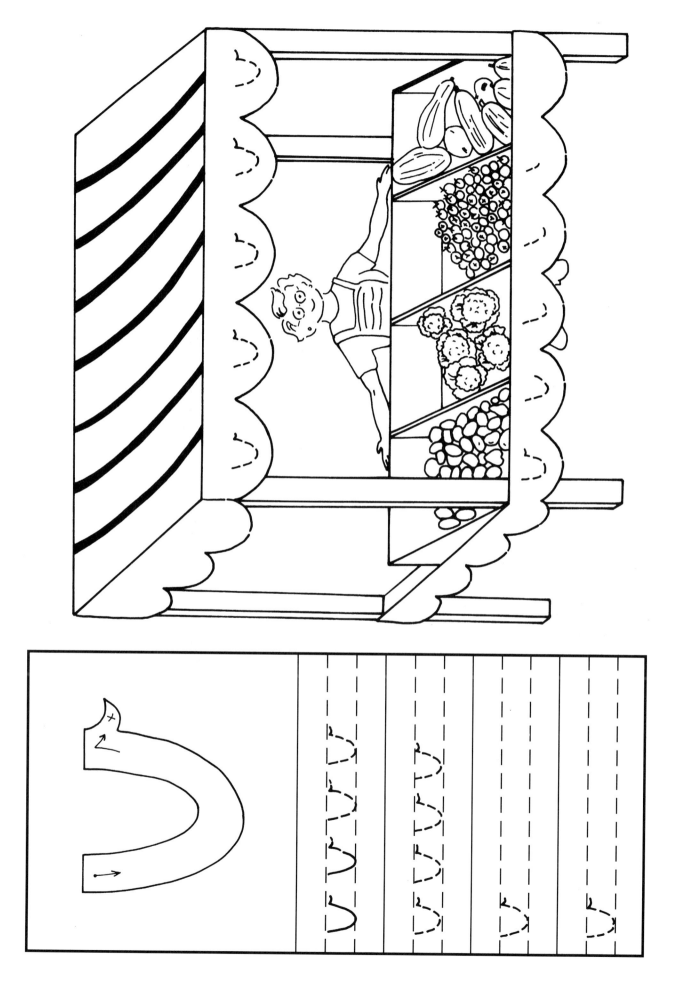

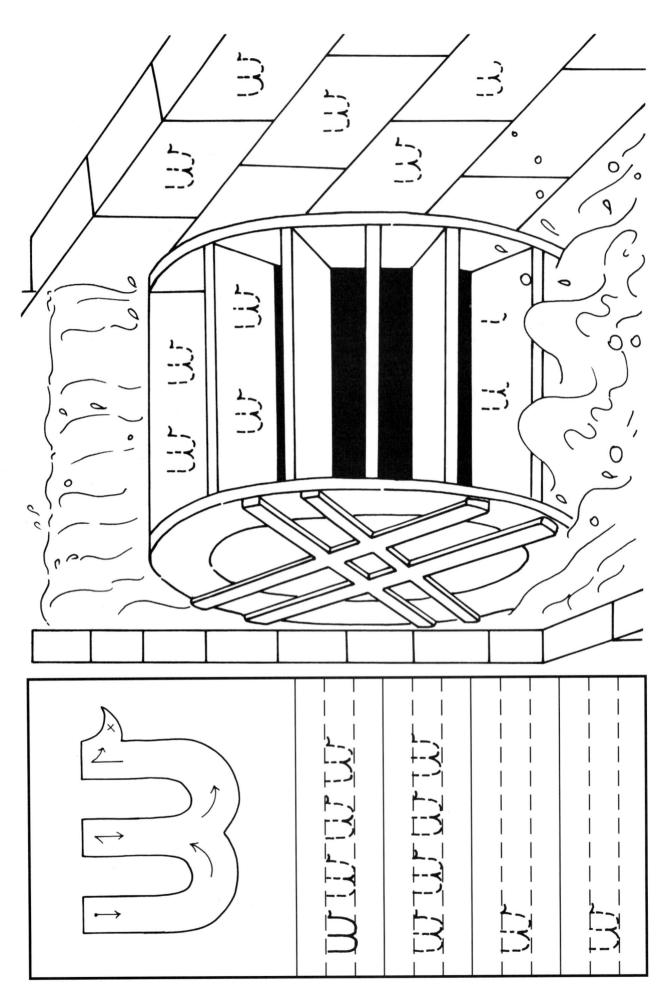

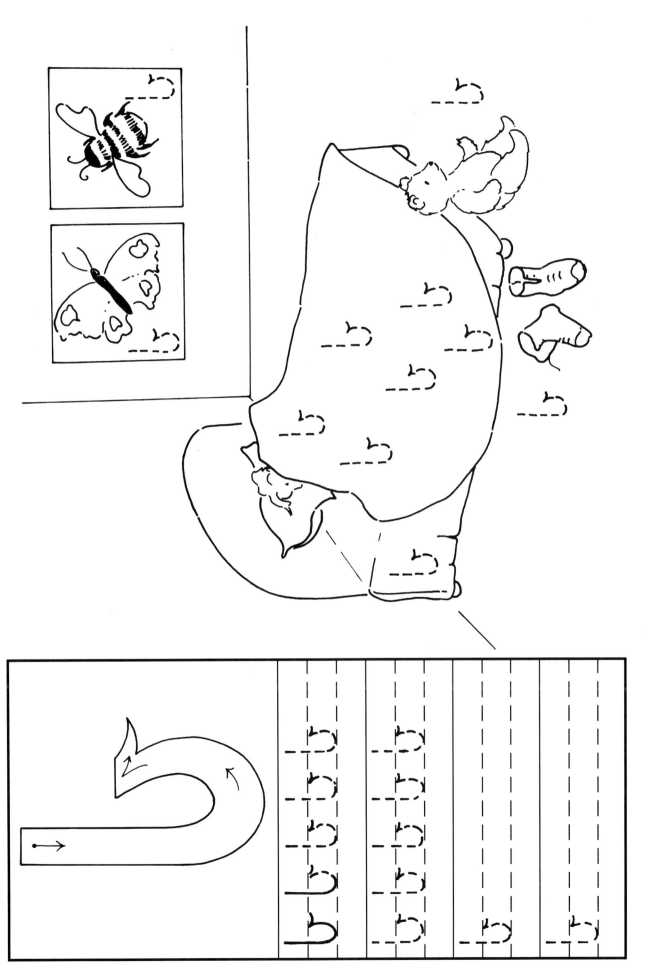

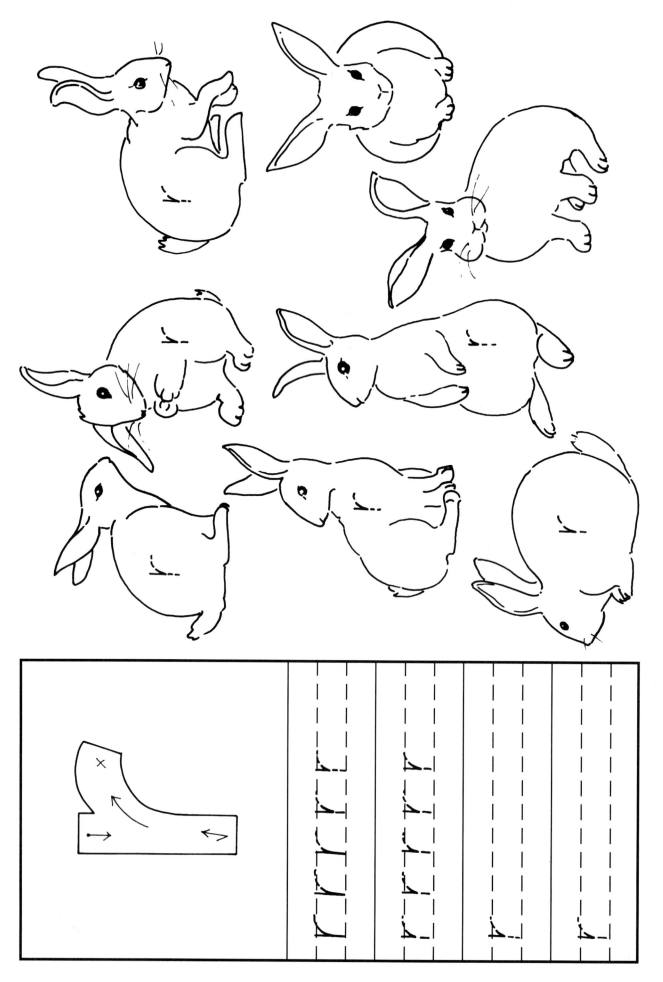

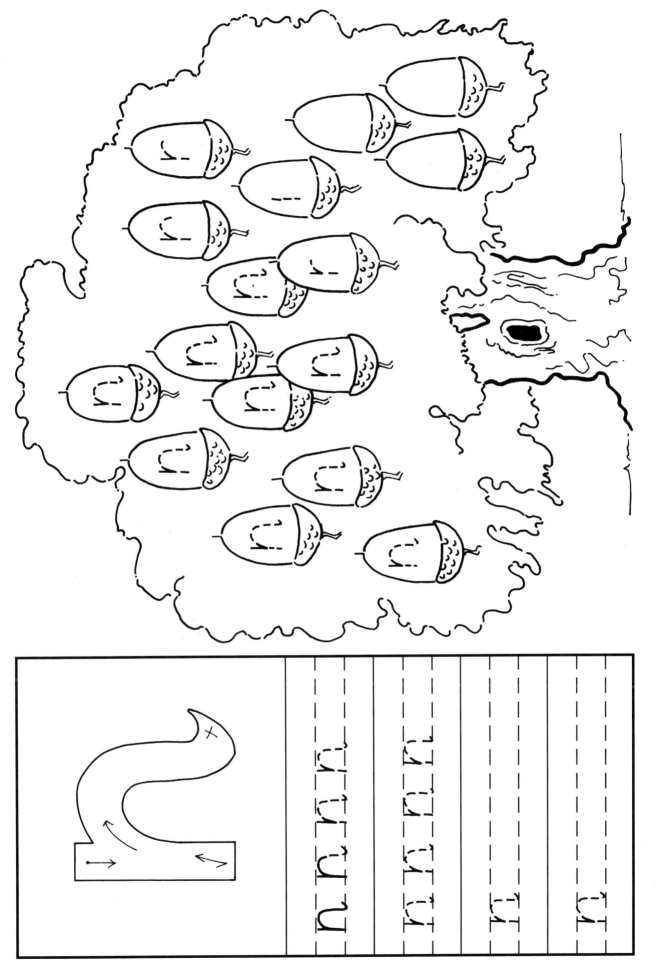

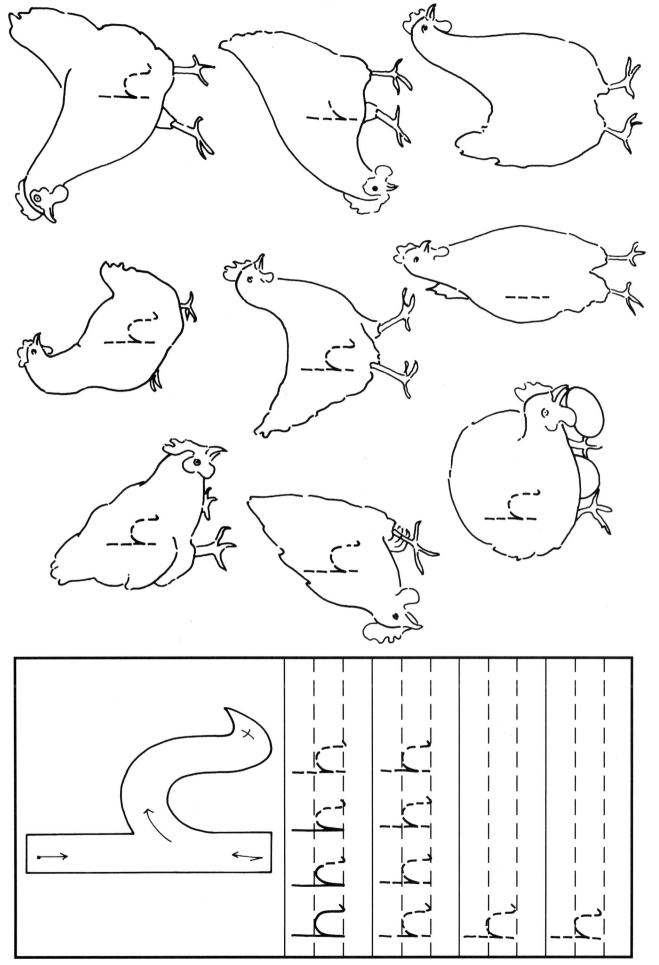

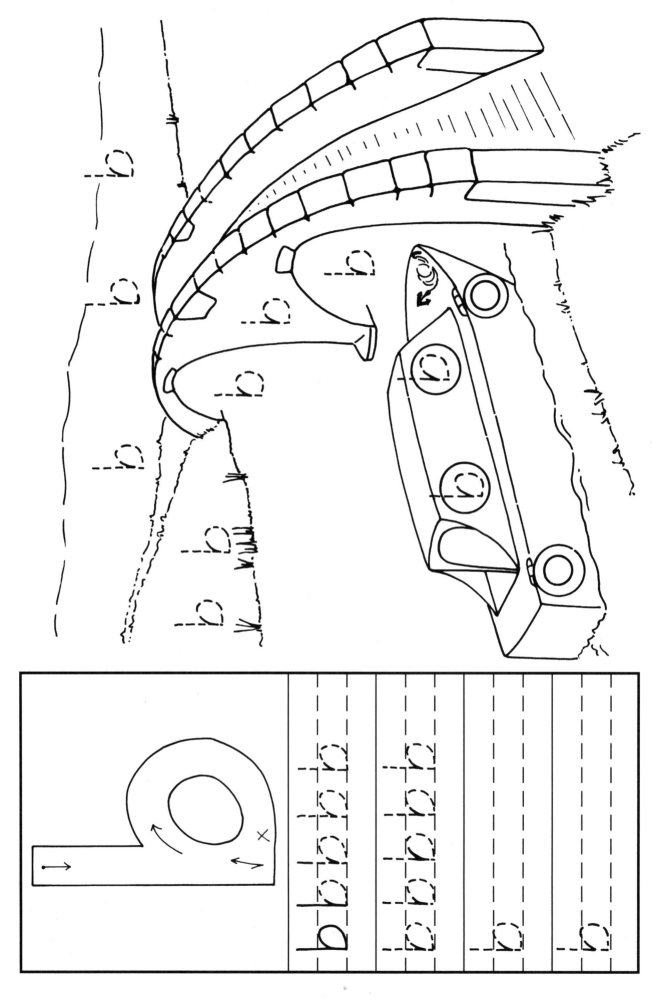

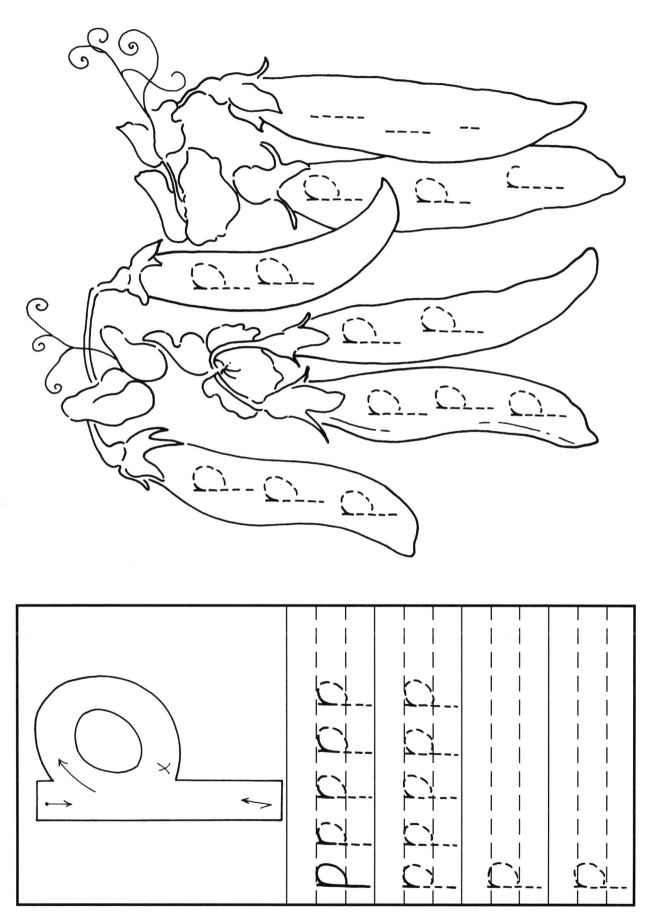

Copymaster 33

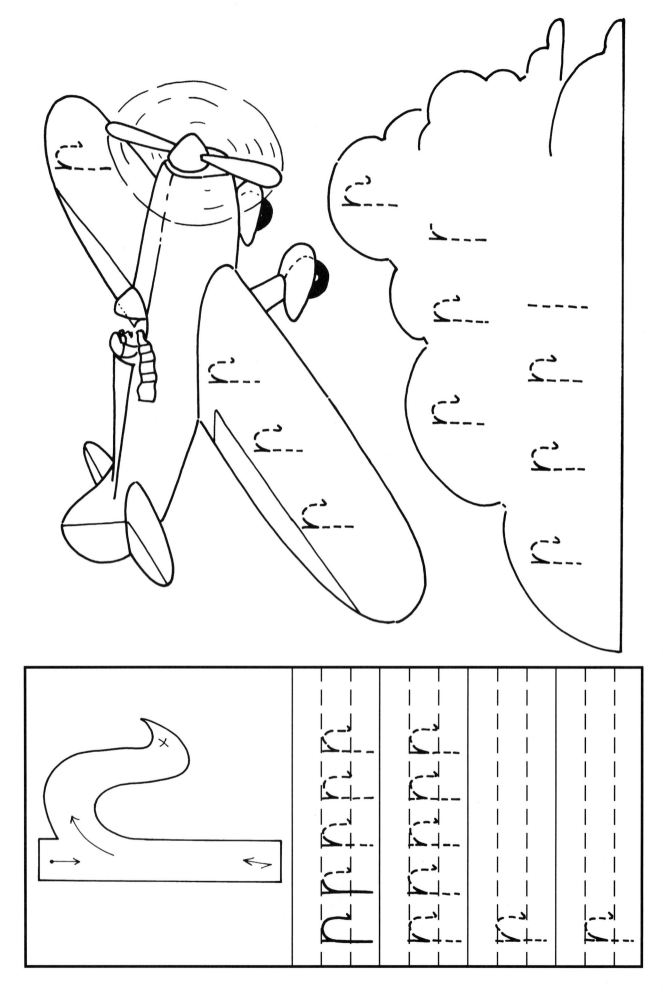

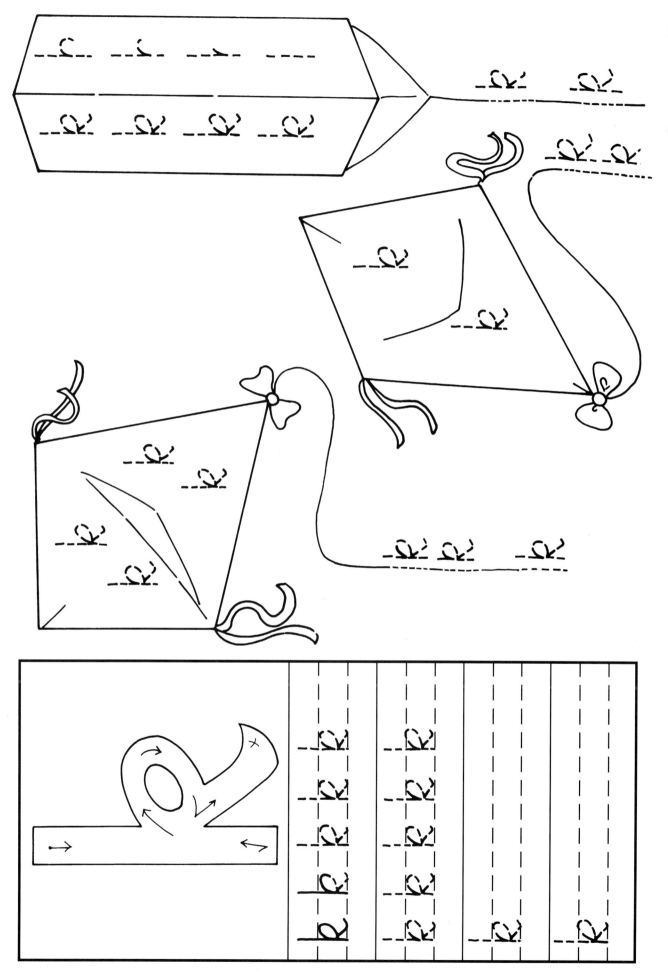

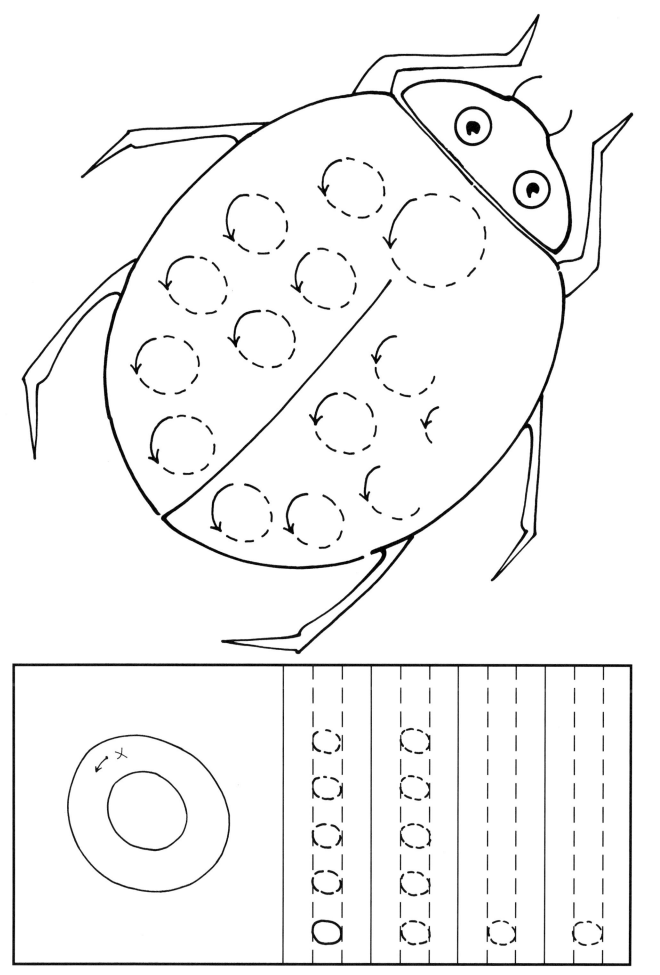

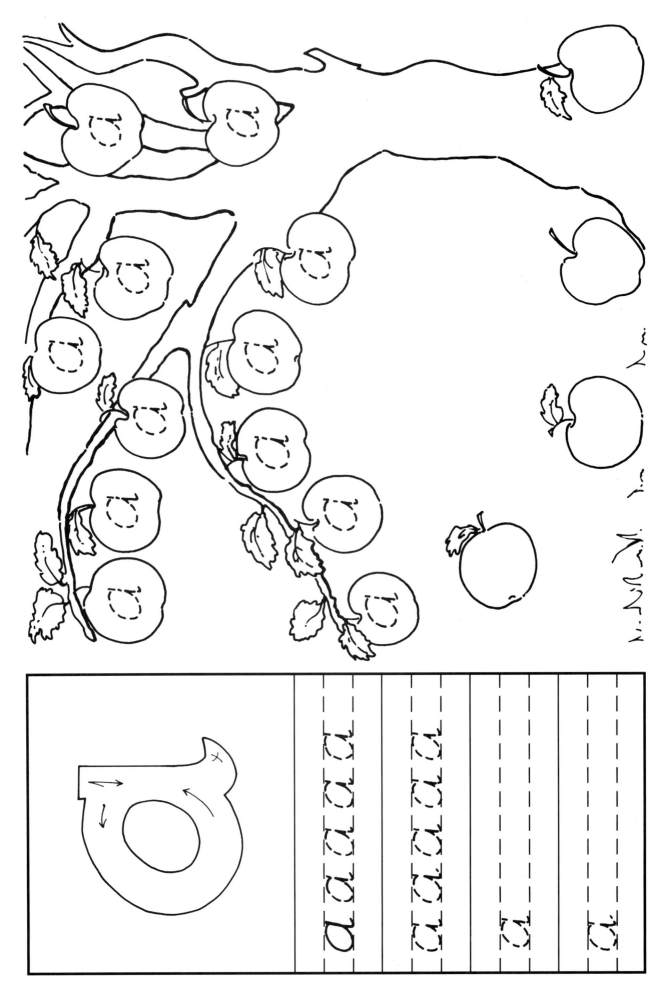

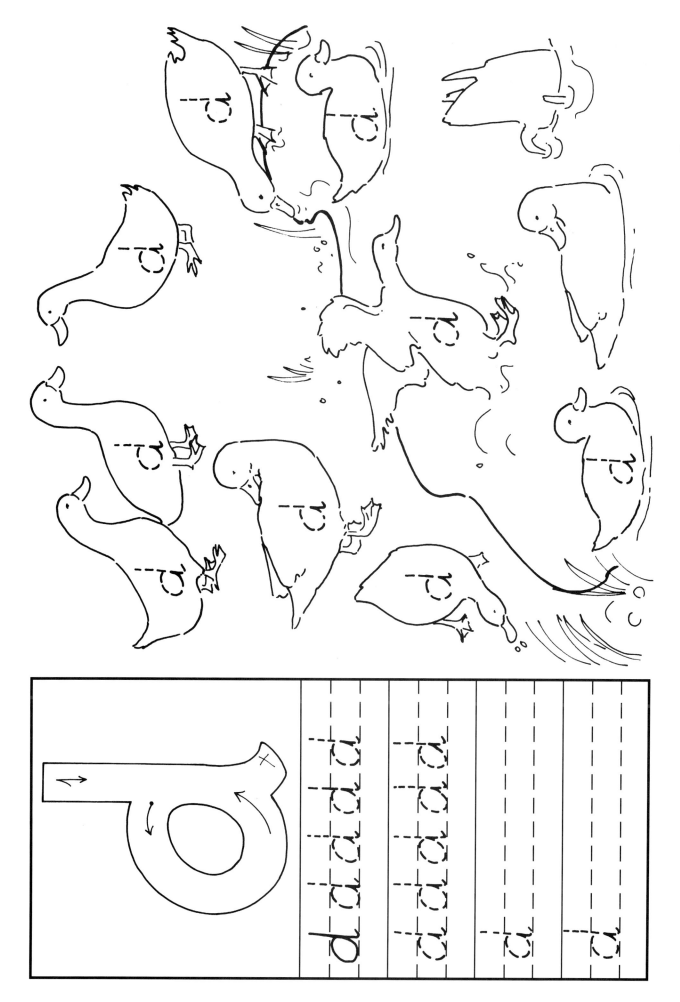

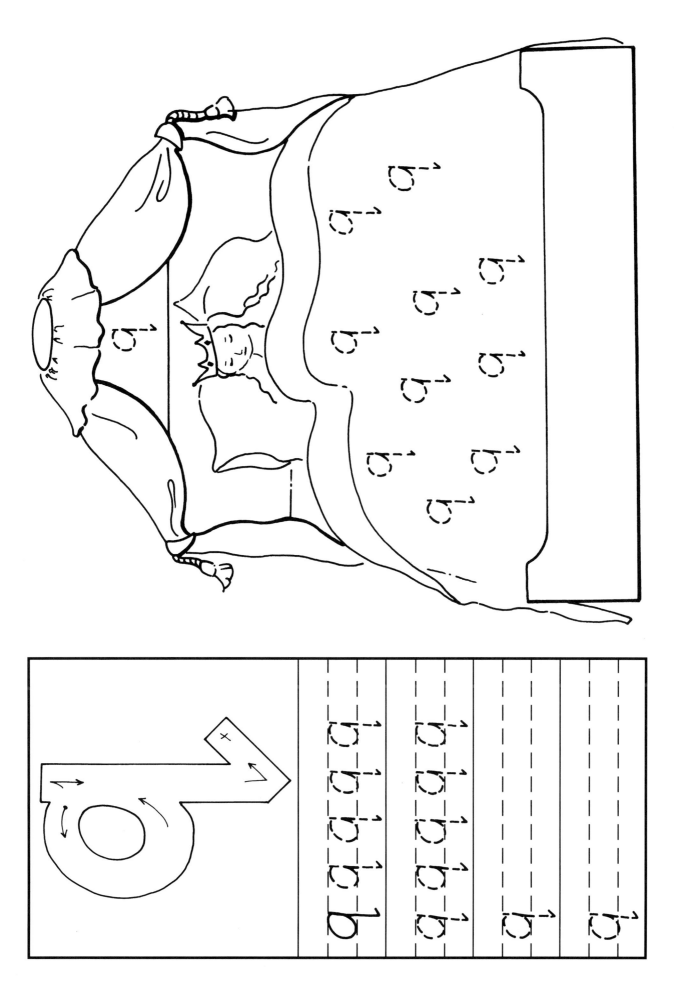

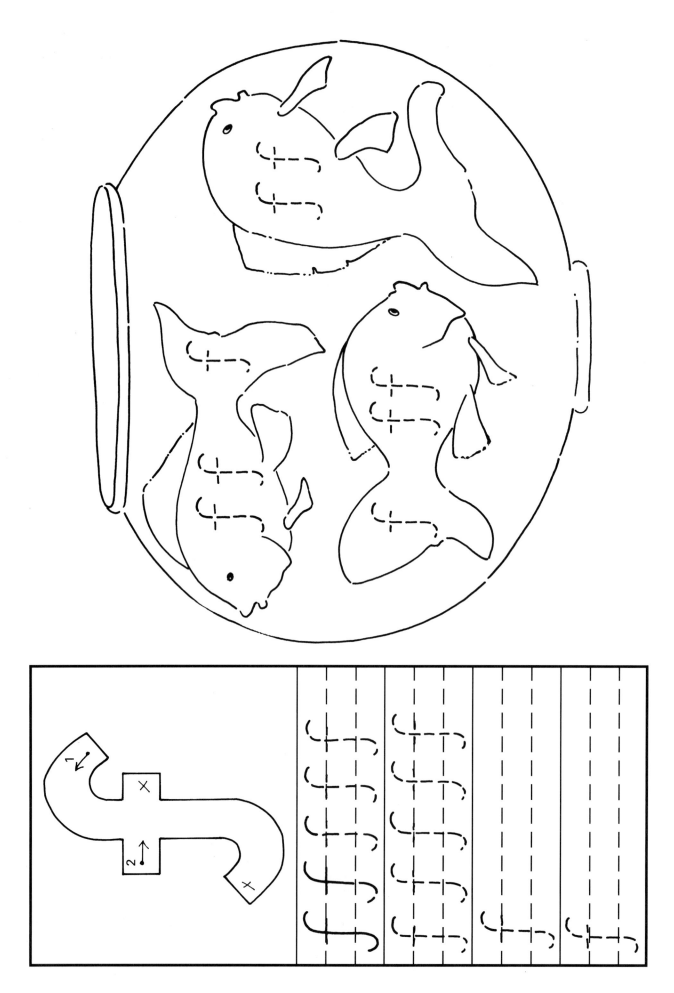

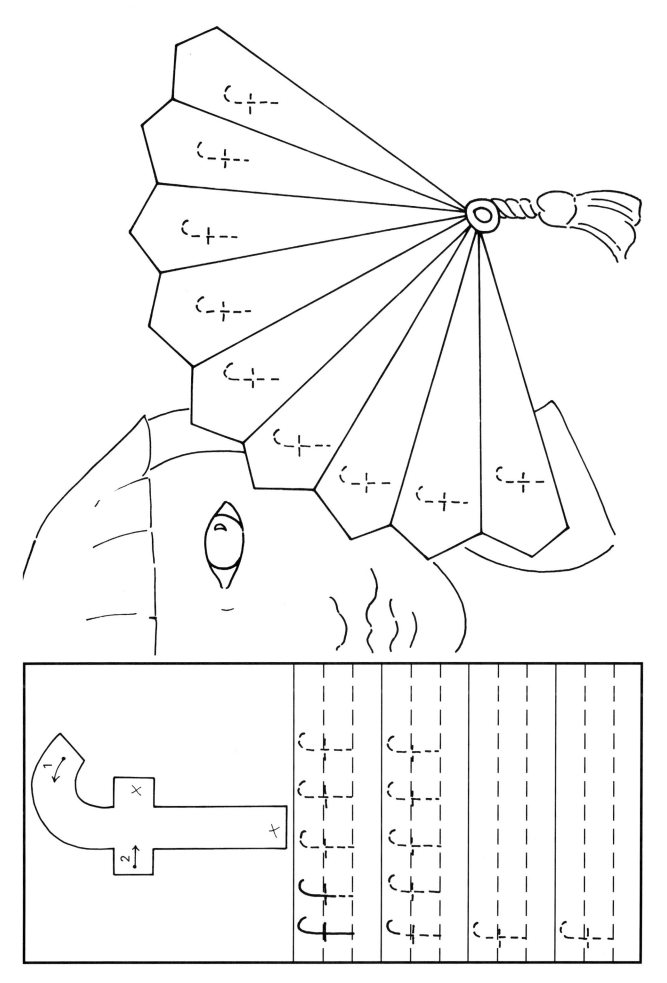

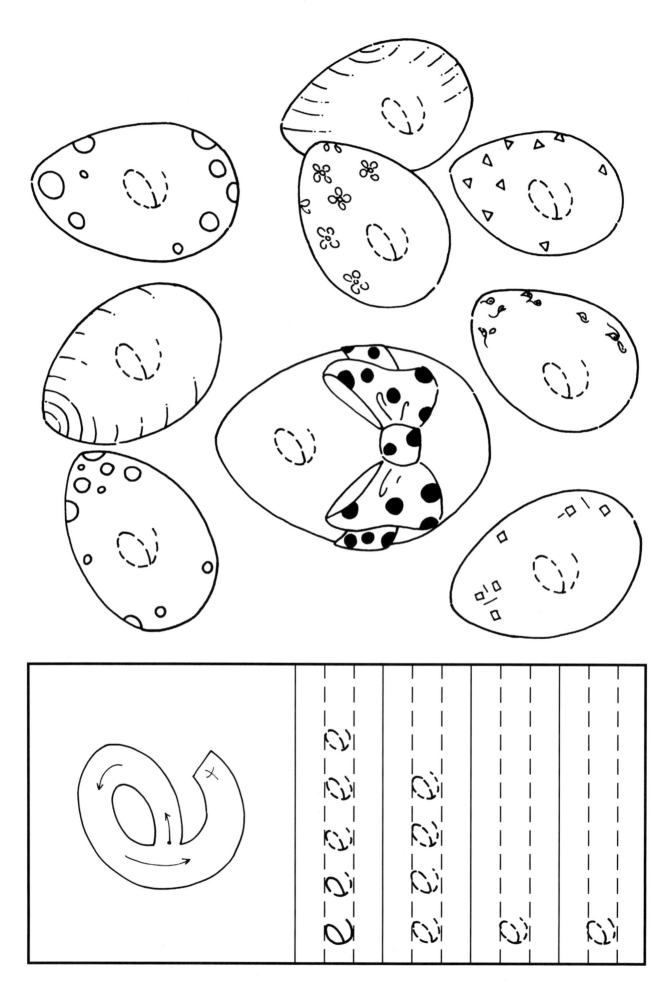

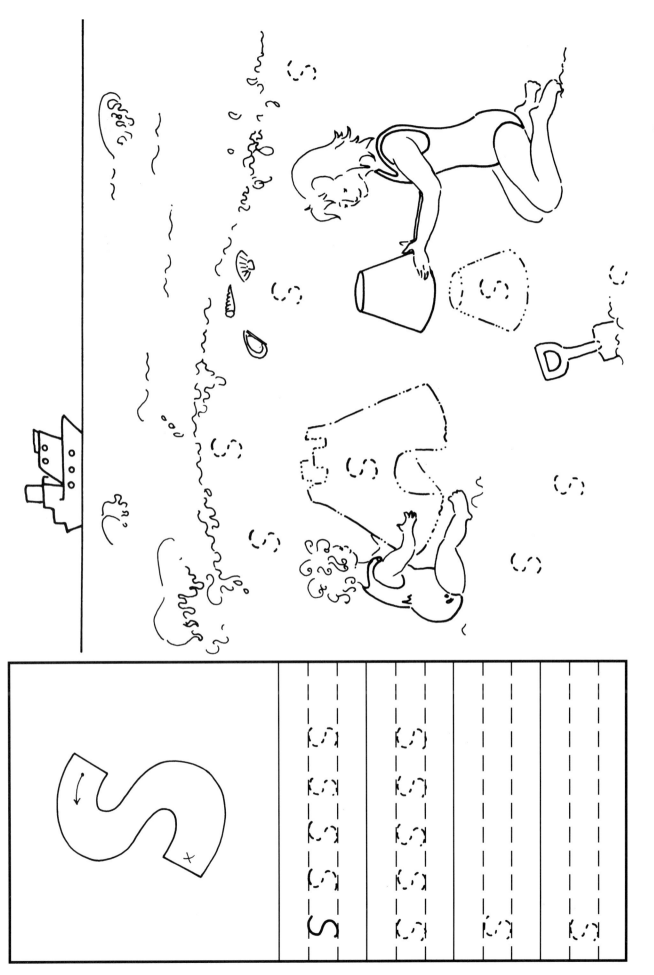

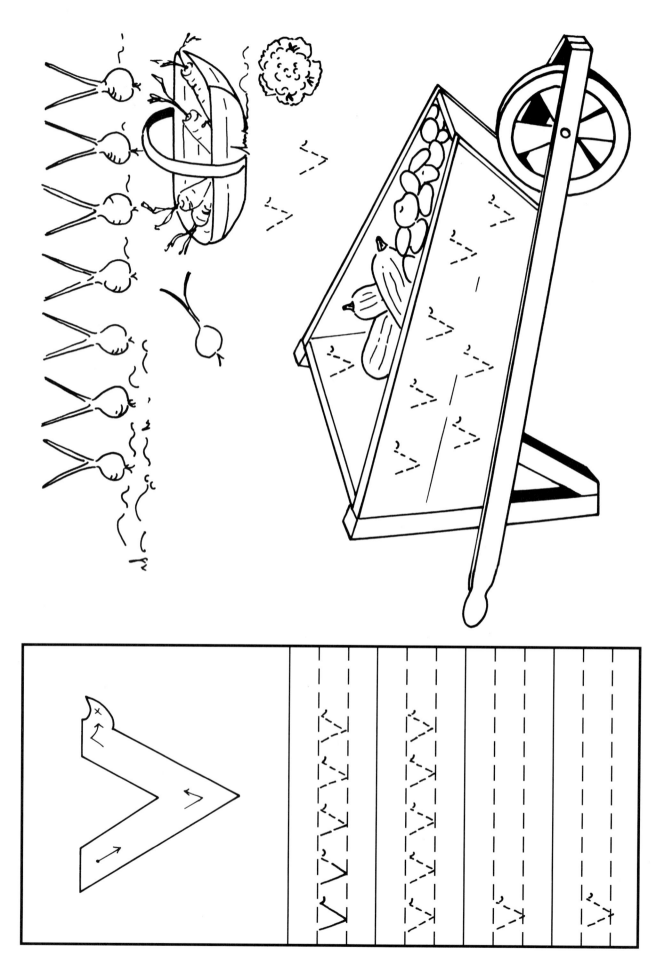

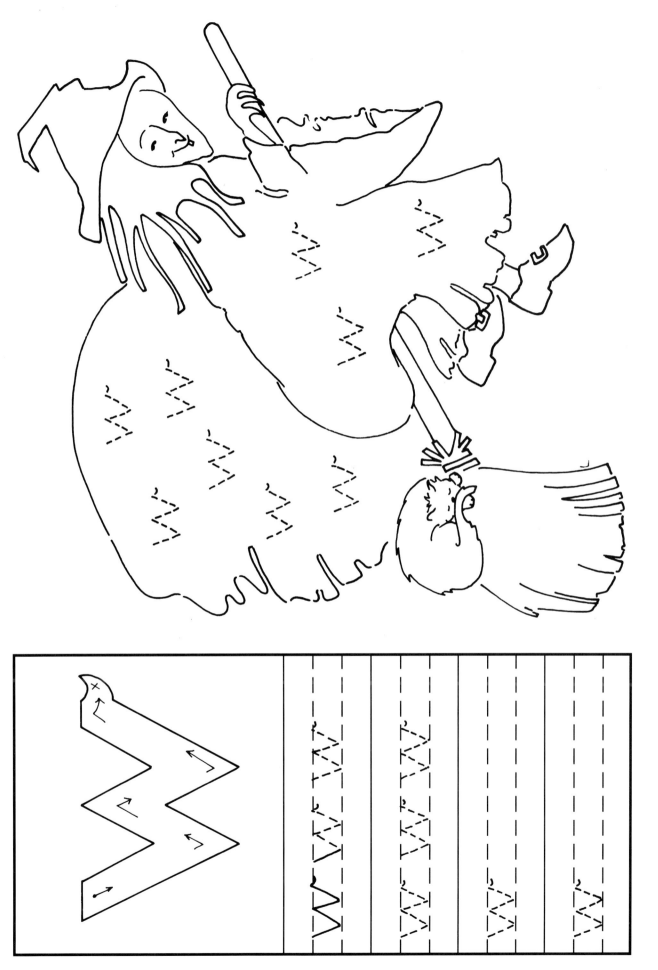

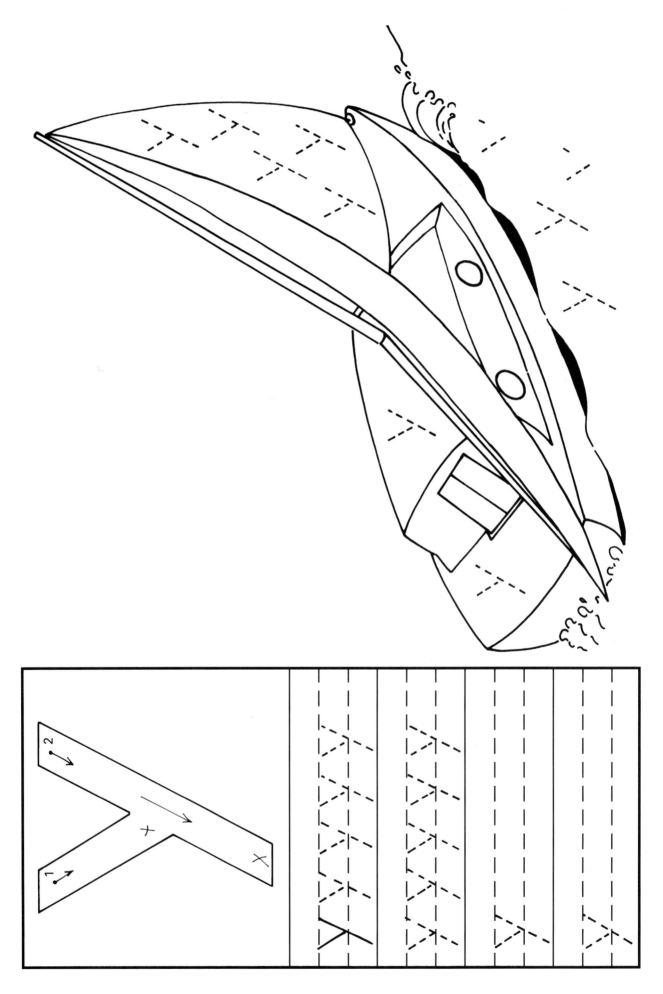

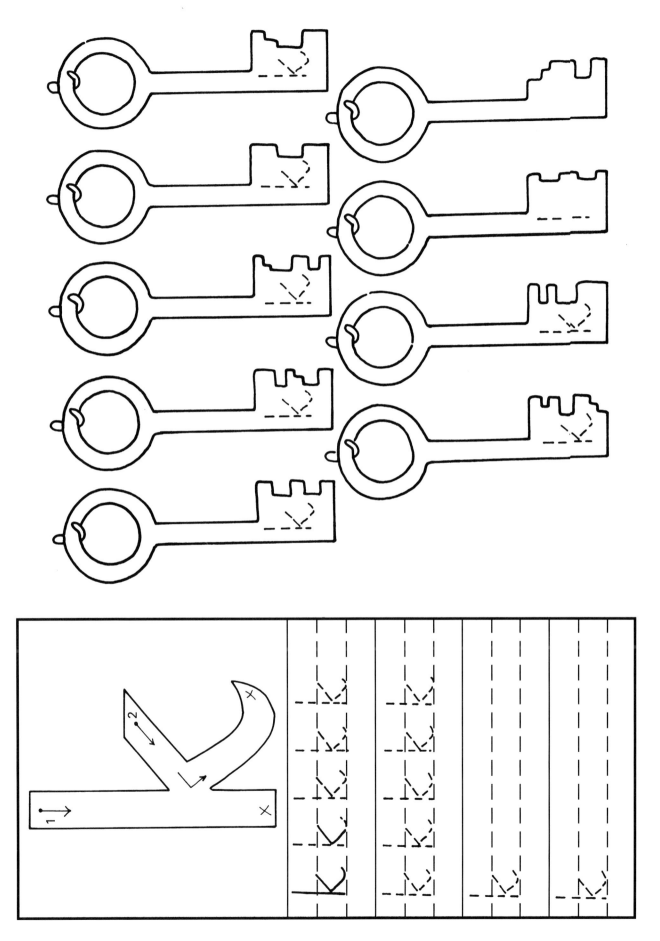

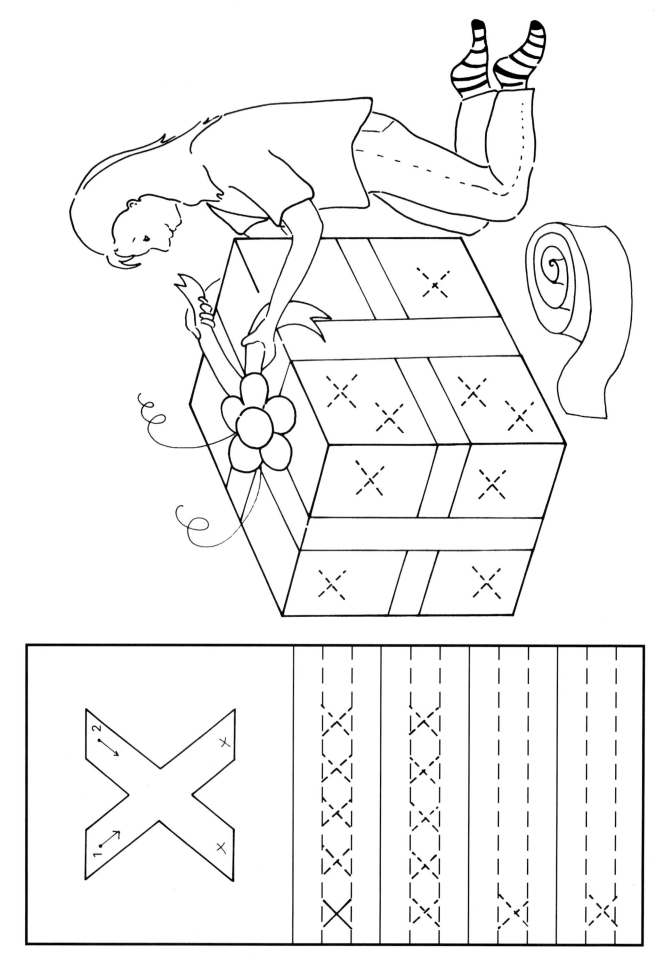

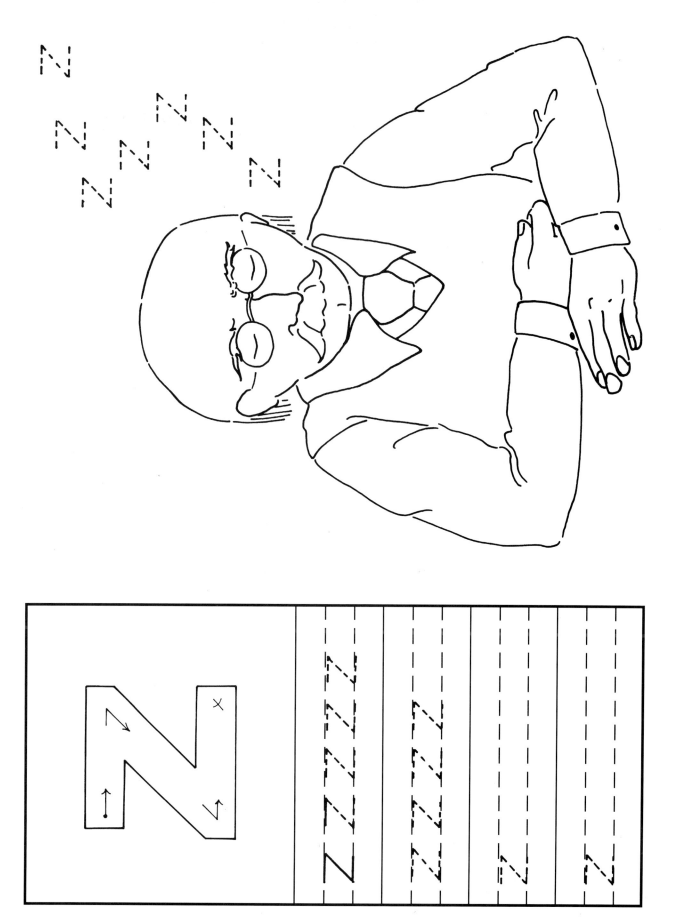

SECTION 3

CAPITALS AND NUMERALS

Copymasters 52–7

Two thirds of capital letters are written with two or more strokes. Most strokes are vertical or horizontal strokes but some letters have an anti-clockwise curve.

The format used in this section gives the children practice in the basic stroke at the top of each sheet before tracing and writing the appropriate capital letter. Dots, arrows, crosses and numbers are again used to indicate the strokes required. Cut the copymasters in half so that children are only focusing on one pair of letters at a time.

Wherever possible letters of similar strokes have been paired up so that the second letter is a development of the first. The sheet for I, L, T, J, is the only copymaster with four letters as each letter forms part of the other.

Copymasters 58–60

The same figure, sitting in a similar position is used for these numeral copymasters. This enables children to see each numeral in relation to the other. They can use parts of the body to remind them of the movements involved to form the numeral . Strokes down or across the body help with positioning. Children can draw the numerals in the air around a seated partner.

Mnemonics are particularly helpful in writing numerals. For example for figure 5 one could say `down his body, round his big fat tummy and put his hat on to keep his tummy dry'. It may sound wordy or even a little twee but it gets all the parts of 5 in the right place. Devise others as necessary with your children. Help them make up their own by asking them what they say to themselves when they are writing a particular numeral. Let them use it as a basis for their own mnemonic and help them to correct it if need be to ensure that the correct movements are being made.

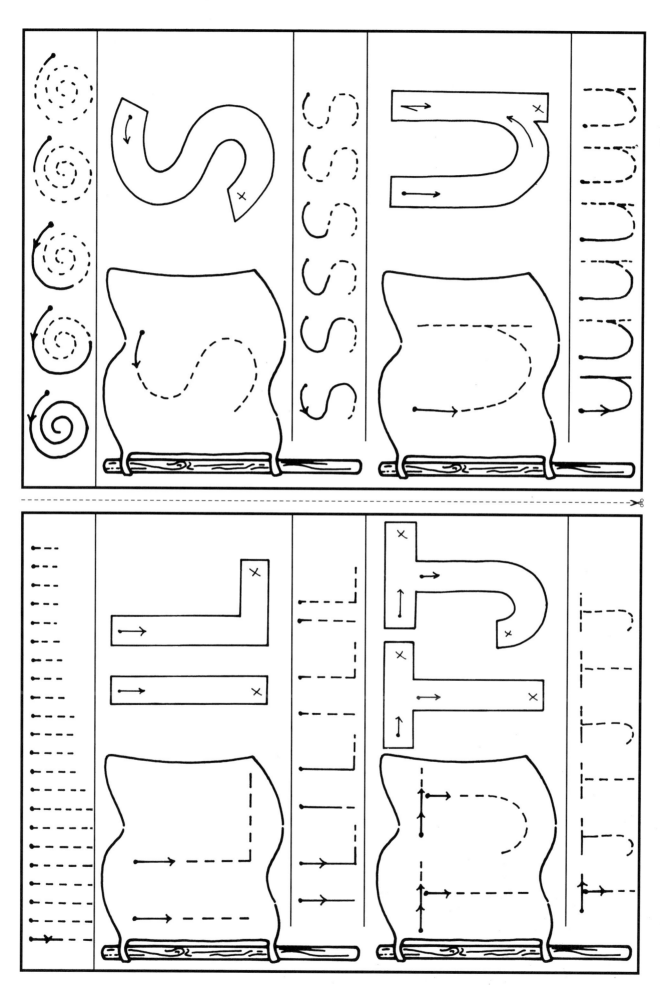

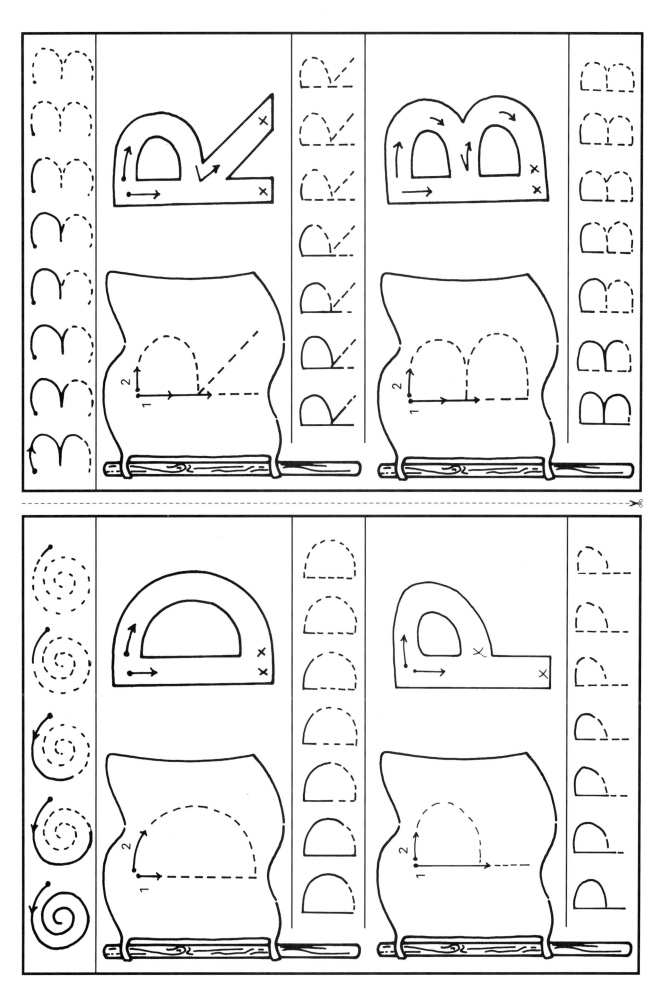

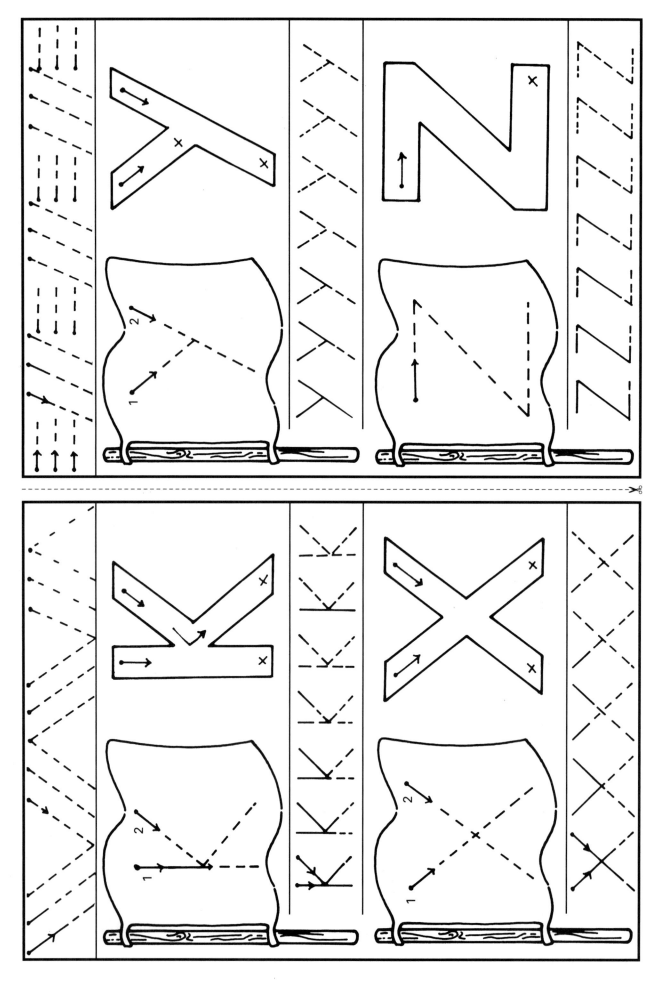

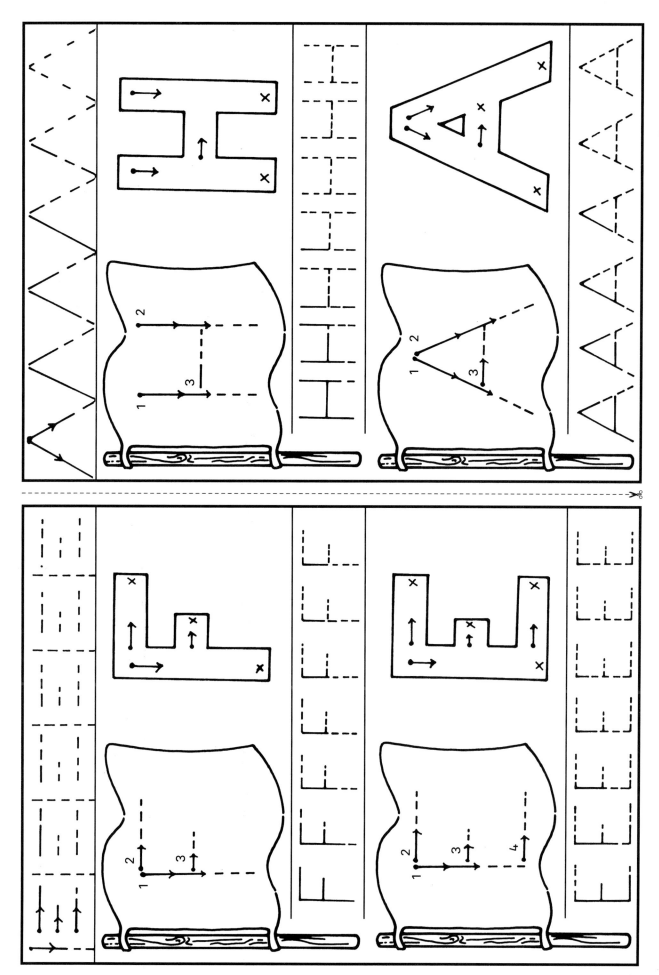

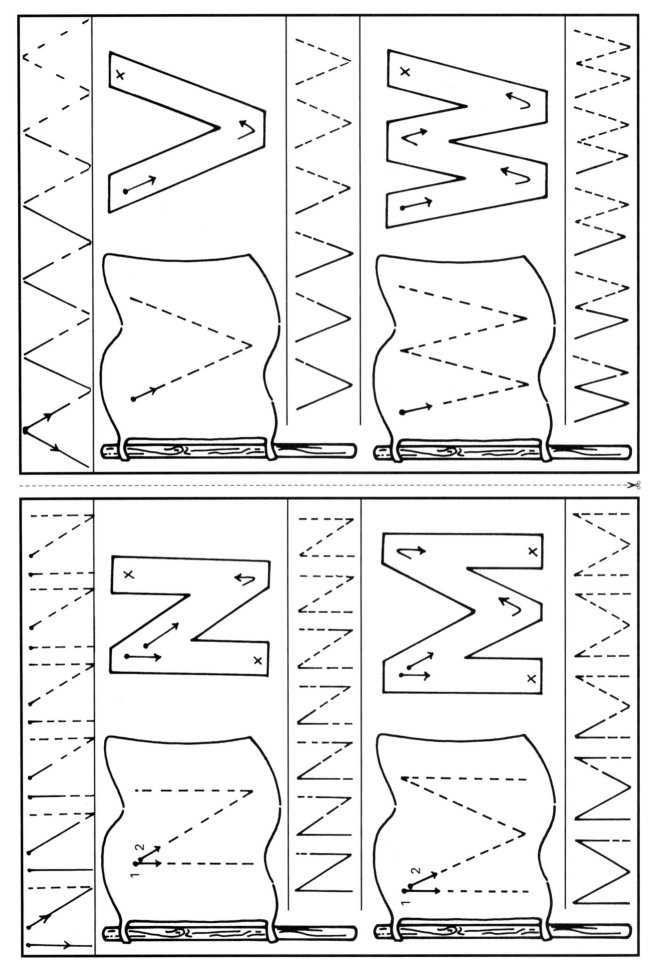

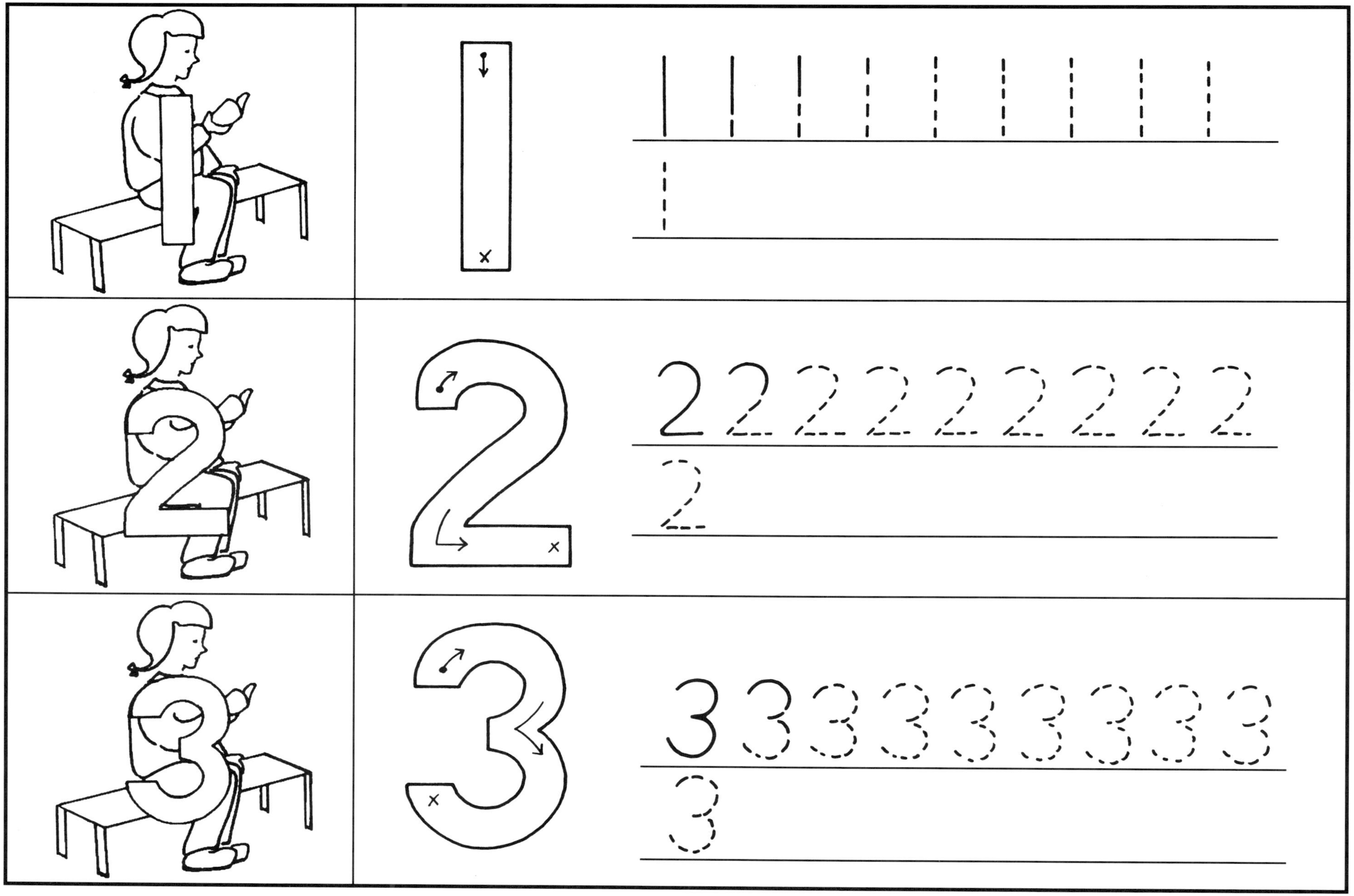

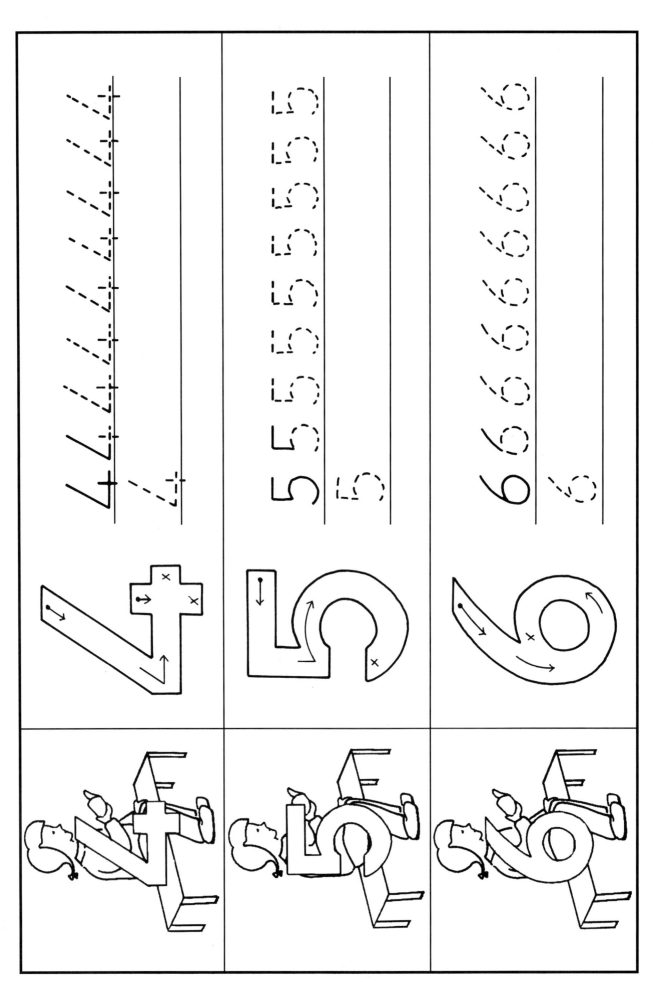

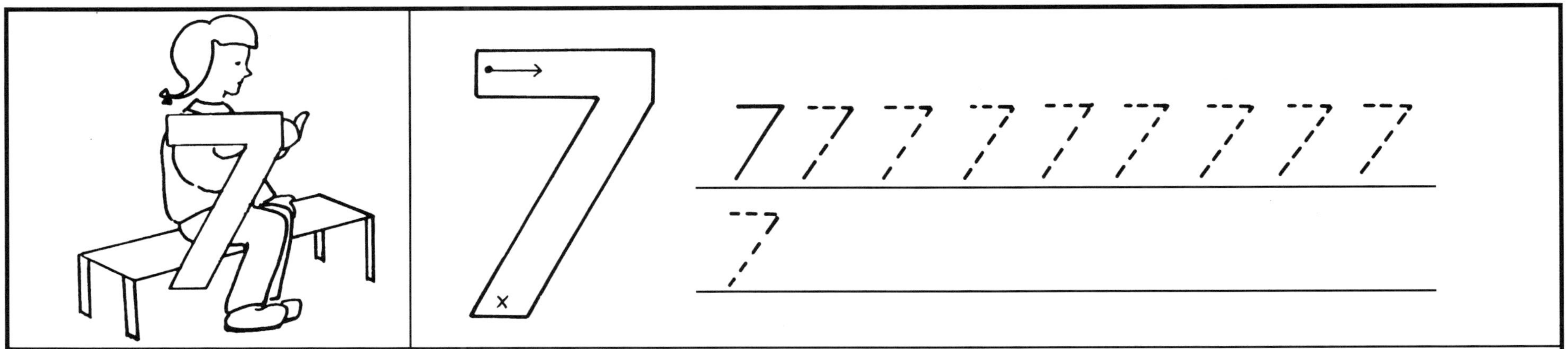

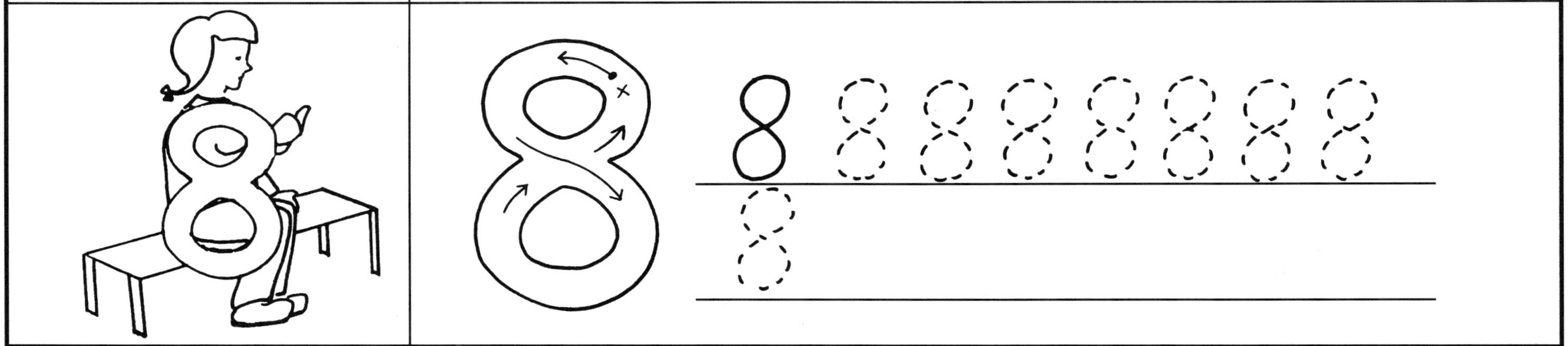

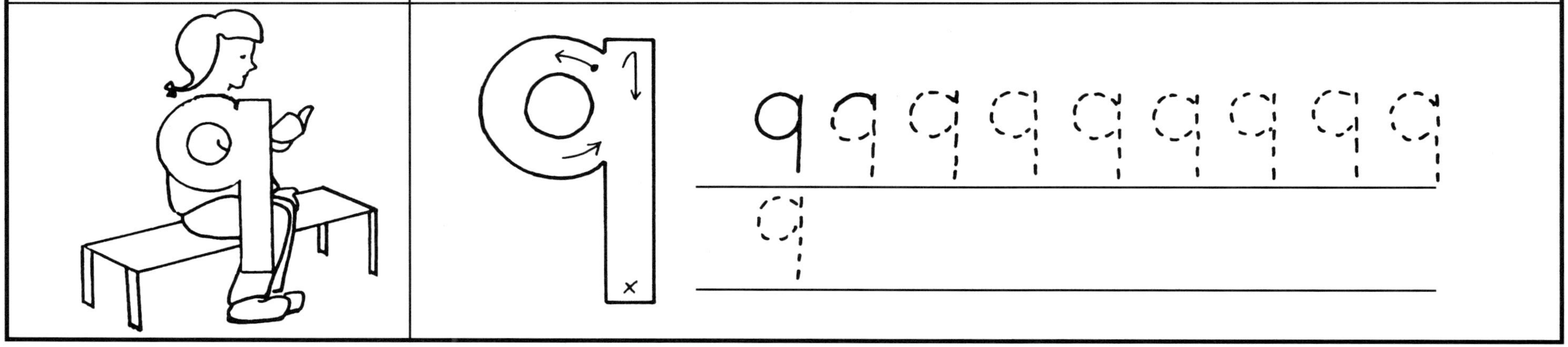

SECTION 4

JOINING LETTERS

In this section we are looking the way letters join together. Wherever possible children should be encouraged to form words without taking their pen or pencil off the paper. This encourages a flowing, speedy style of writing. It is also extremely helpful for children who have spelling problems, or are dyslexic, to write the whole word in one continuous movement.

Basically there are two kinds of joins, diagonal – where the joining strokes comes from the bottom of the letter – and horizontal – where the join comes from the top. Children have practised exit strokes in the previous section so they will know where the join commences. Some children will already have begun to make joins because, in most cases, it is merely by extending the exit strokes that letters become joined.

Practising has an important role to play in handwriting because it trains our muscle memory how to write a letter or word. Muscle memory is central to our lives. It is through practising a motor movement that we store the movement in our memories. If we repeat one or more movements often enough our response will become automatic. We develop an automatic response to opening a book, buttoning a shirt or washing our hands. We do these actions without thinking about them. It is the same with handwriting. Once a letter or word shape is stored in our muscle memory we do not have to think about how to do it when we want to write it down.

On each copymaster a box displays a letter with its particular join showing it large and bold with directional arrows to indicate the movements. Children should both visually track and finger trace the letter in the box before going on to the patterns in the picture and then the words on the training lines.

Some of the pictures are vehicles for the letter shape like the tiles on the well in Copymaster 61 whilst others support the letter both visually and aurally like the clown in Copymaster 63. On the picture the letter joining with itself is practised as well as some of the common joins it makes with letters already covered in this section.

The words in the training lines contain only letters which use the joining movements already learnt and provide space for children to copy the word. The word should be copied in many different ways as suggested before to really fix the movement in a child's memory.

Letter changes are introduced for letters 'z' on Copymaster 71, 'r' on Copymaster 73 and and copymasters provided for two forms of the letters 'b', 'f', 'v' 'w' and 'x'. Select the ones which are closest to your school's scheme. Should minor changes need to be made to a letter, e.g. if you prefer not to join 'b' or 's', use correction fluid to blot out the join on the copymaster before copying it.

DIAGONAL JOINS

All letters which finish on the base line join other letters with a diagonal ligature.

Copymasters 61–3
These three copymasters deal with families of letters, those formed from a 'u' shape like 'i, 'l' and 'u'; those from a tunnel like 'n, 'm' and 'h'; those from an anti-clockwise movement like 'c', 'o' and 'd'.

Copymaster 64
This sheet deals with 'e' when the join is diagonal. The up stroke for the 'e' is an extension of the exit stroke from the previous letter. *led*
A minor change occurs in 'e' when the previous stroke is a horizontal join. *red*

Examples of both joins are in words on Copymasters 73–6.

Copymaster 65
The letter 's' shown here begins with a diagonal stroke *os* . This makes for a smooth flowing join where 's' follows a letter with a baseline exit stroke, a diagonal join. This letter shape easily adapts to a horizontal join such as: *os*
If you prefer 's' to keep its script shape see Copymaster 66.

Copymaster 67
Here 'b' keeps its script shape and joins from the base with a diagonal join. If you prefer 'b' not to join blot out

88

the join before photocopying. If you prefer this ʋ shape for '**b**', (which prevents '**b**' and '**d**' reversals and is more flowing) see Copymaster 77.

Copymaster 68
The letter '**k**' is written in one continuous movement. If you prefer it to be formed from two strokes adapt the copymaster accordingly.

Copymaster 69
Letter '**f**' is shown here as one flowing movement. If you

prefer '**f**' to join from its cross bar please see Copymaster 75.

Copymaster 70
Letter '**q**' is one of the few letters whose descender joins from below the line.

Copymaster 74
Here '**z**' is shown joining from a looped descender. You may prefer to join directly from a script '**z**'. ᴢᴏᴏ If you do, insist that the sharp corners to the letter are preserved.

HORIZONTAL JOINTS

All letters which finish at the top of the 'x' height join other letters with a horizontal ligature. The ligature should dip slightly to help keep the flowing movement.

With more letters available many of the practice words are taken from those which children use most often and need to commit to memory.

Copymaster 72
This copymaster shown '**o**' paired with both minims and ascenders. The ligature should still have a slight dip even when joined to an ascender. ᴏᴏ ᴏh

Copymaster 73
Letter '**r**' changes shape at the top to accommodate the join. Make sure that the up stroke does not split away until halfway up otherwise it quickly comes to look like a script '**v**'.

Copymaster 74
Here letters '**v**' and '**w**' are the cursive form which is flowing and easy to write. They join in the same way and dip the ligature on joining. Ensure that the middle stroke of '**w**' is the same height as the outer two strokes. ᴜʋ

Copymaster 75
The copymaster shows the form of '**f**' where it joins

horizontally from the cross bar. Ensure that the down stroke is straight not leaning backwards nor twisting from left to right. The most difficult part of this letter is when two '**f**'s are written together. If not written with care '**ff**' can look very ugly.

Copymaster 76
Letters '**v**' and '**w**' are shown here in the script form. If you use this form make sure that the points are kept sharp or the letters will deteriorate into a squiggle. ᴡ

Copymaster 77
The cursive form of '**b**' is used here closed slightly at the top to give it form. It has a flowing smooth movement. Its shape ensures that there is no 'b-d' confusion. ʋ-d

Copymaster 78
This sheet has two versions of '**x**'. You may prefer to join '**x**' like this axe as it makes a smooth join to a diagonal. The majority of joins are diagonal.

Copymaster 79
Children sometimes find it difficult to cope with non-joining letters especially in the middle of a word. This page gives examples of how to cope with '**g**', '**j**' and '**y**'.

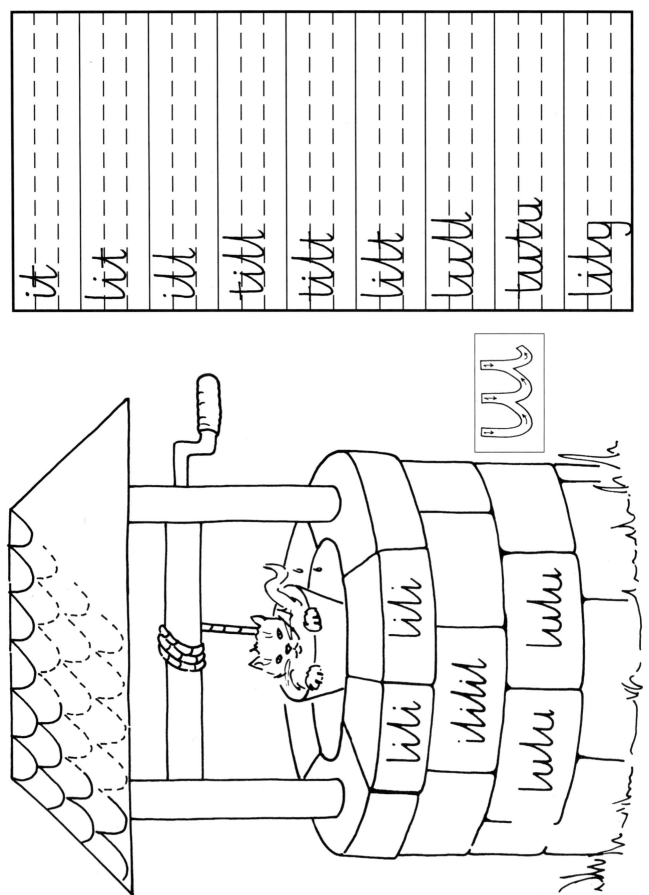

it

lit

itt

titt

titt

litt

lutt

tutu

litty

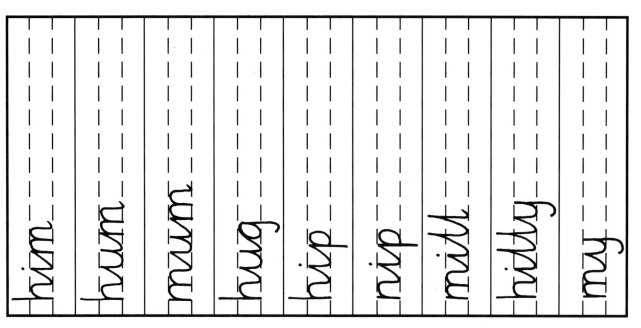

him

hum

mum

hug

hip

nip

mitt

hilly

my

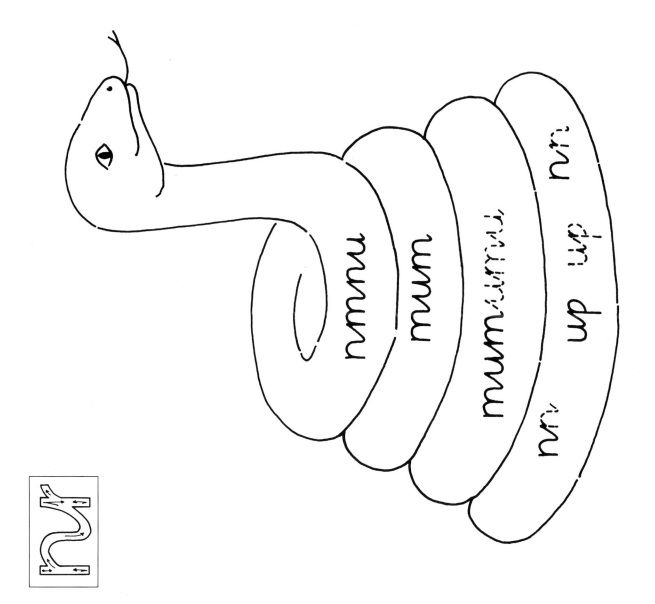

cat

can

and

had

dad

cut

call

chip

that

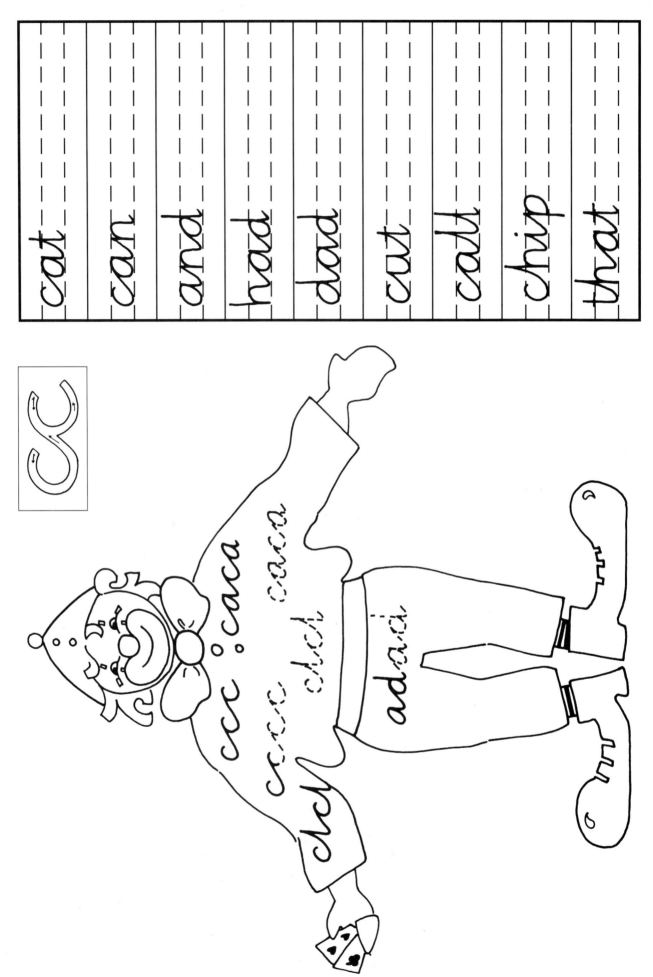

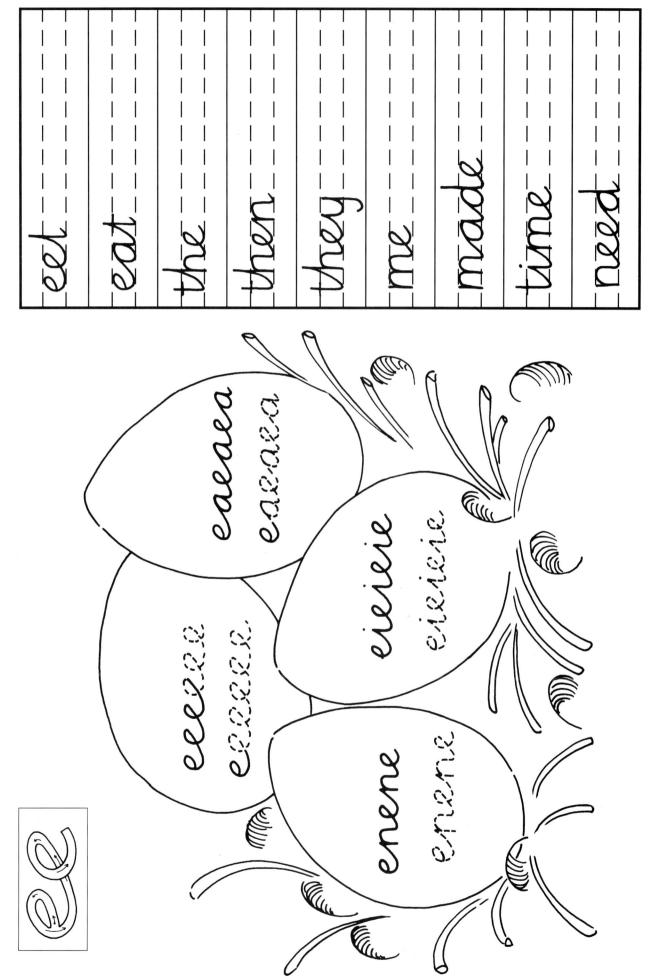

eet

eat

the

then

they

me

made

time

need

ee

eaeaea

eieie

enene

is

this

has

us

she

see

said

ship

mass

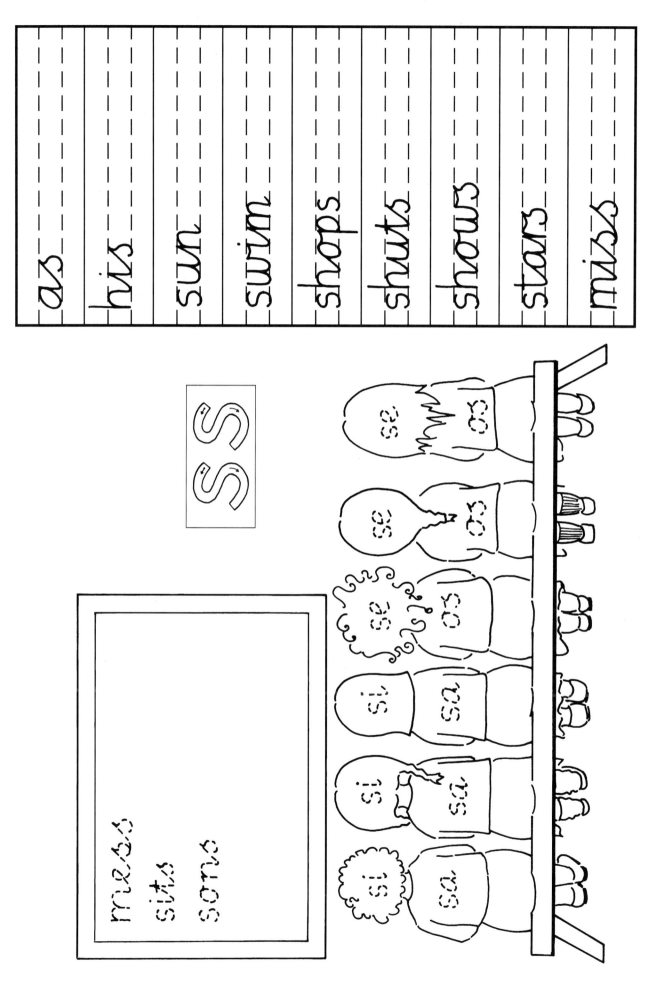

as

his

sun

swim

shops

shuts

shows

stars

miss

s s

mess

sits

sons

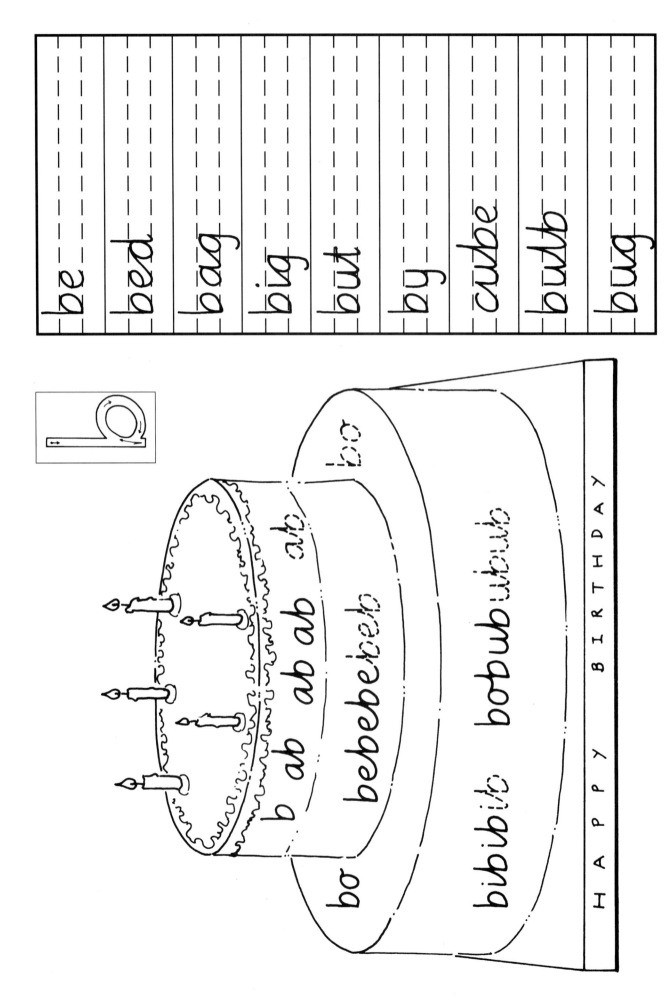

be

bed

bag

big

but

by

cube

bulb

bug

b

b ab ab ab ab

bebebebeb

bibibib

bo

ba

bobubub

HAPPY BIRTHDAY

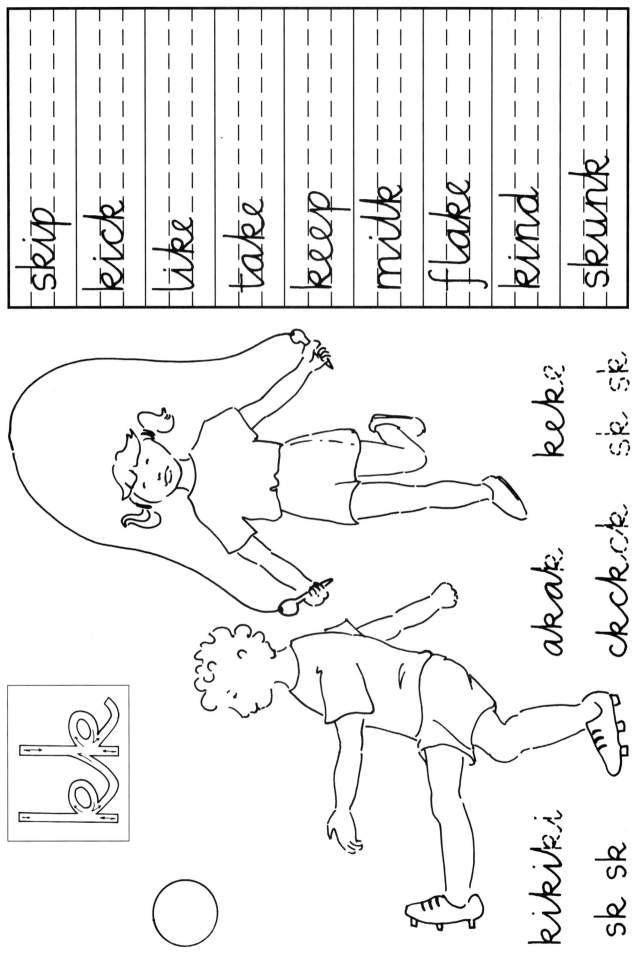

skip

kick

like

take

keep

milk

flake

kind

skunk

keke
sk sk

akak
ckckck

kikiki
sk sk

fat

fed

fin

full

fee

off

after

fluffy

fling

fe fi fo fum

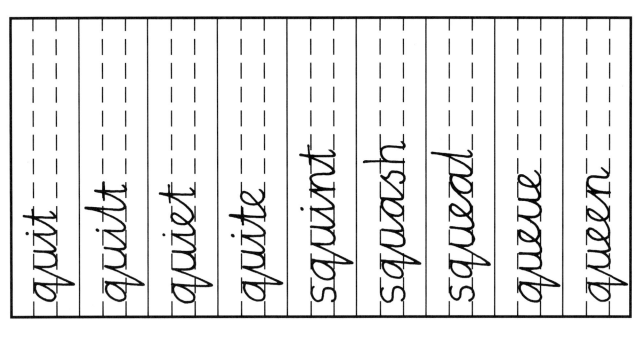

qu

quit

quilt

quiet

quite

squint

squash

squeal

queue

queen

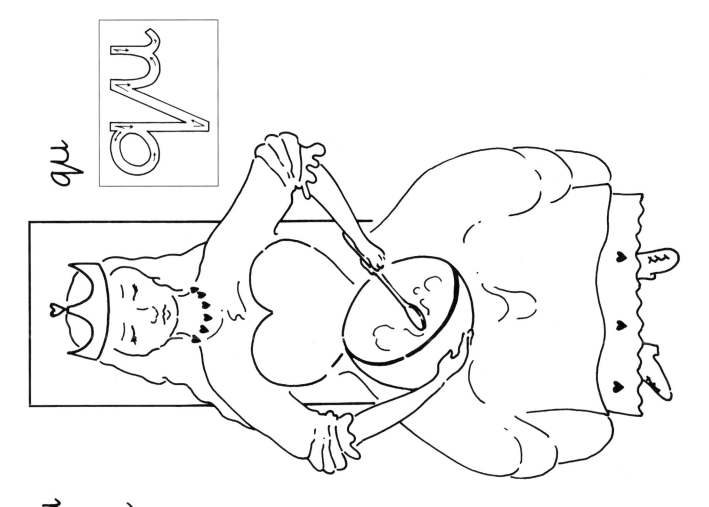

quau
quau
squ
squ

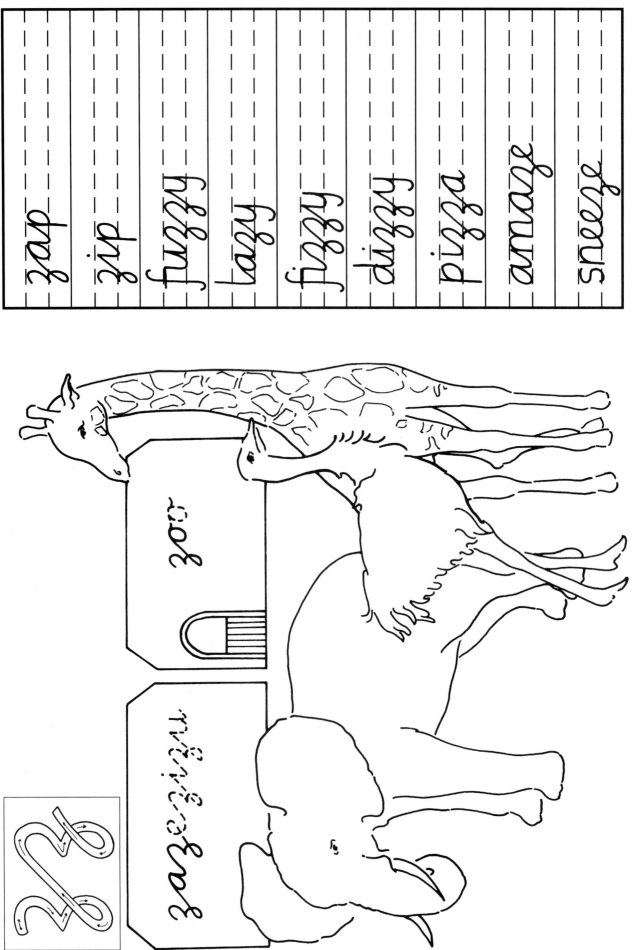

zap

zip

fuzzy

lazy

fizzy

dizzy

pizza

amaze

sneeze

zoo

zag-zig-zu

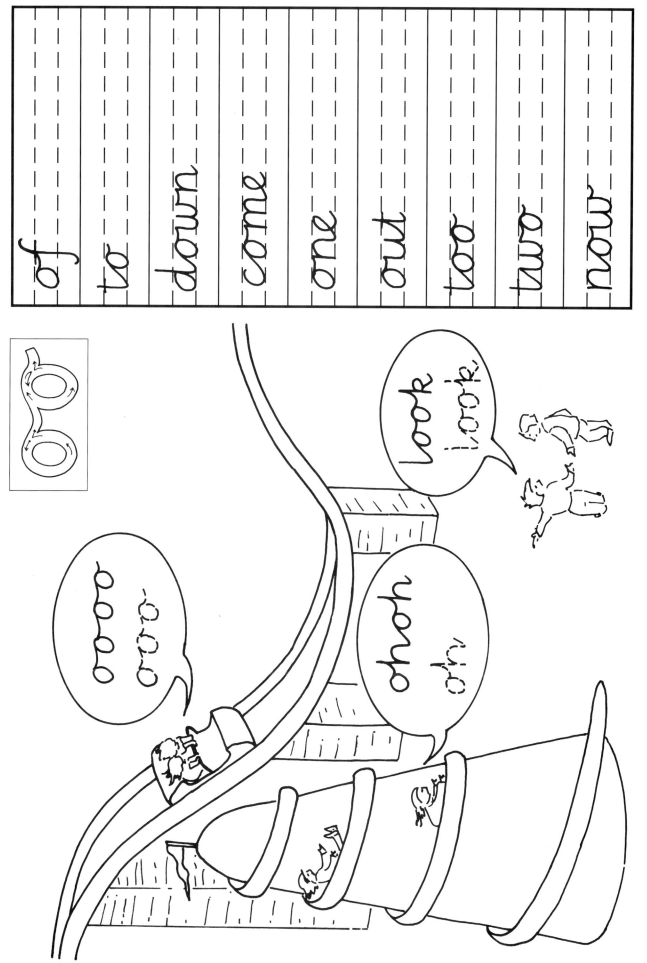

ran

rent

rip

roll

are

her

there

from

hurry

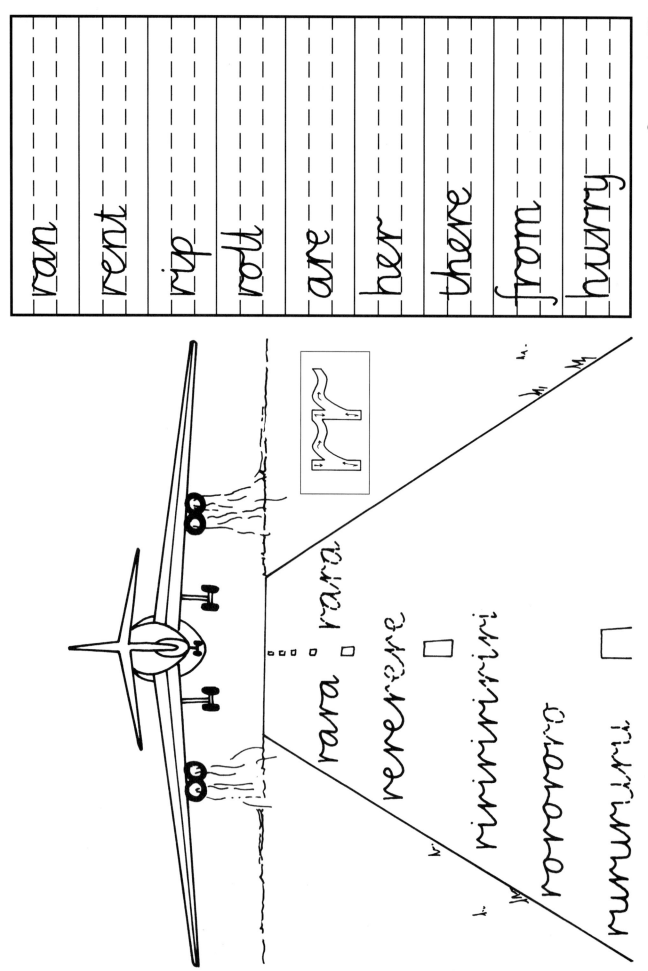

rara rara

rerere

rororo

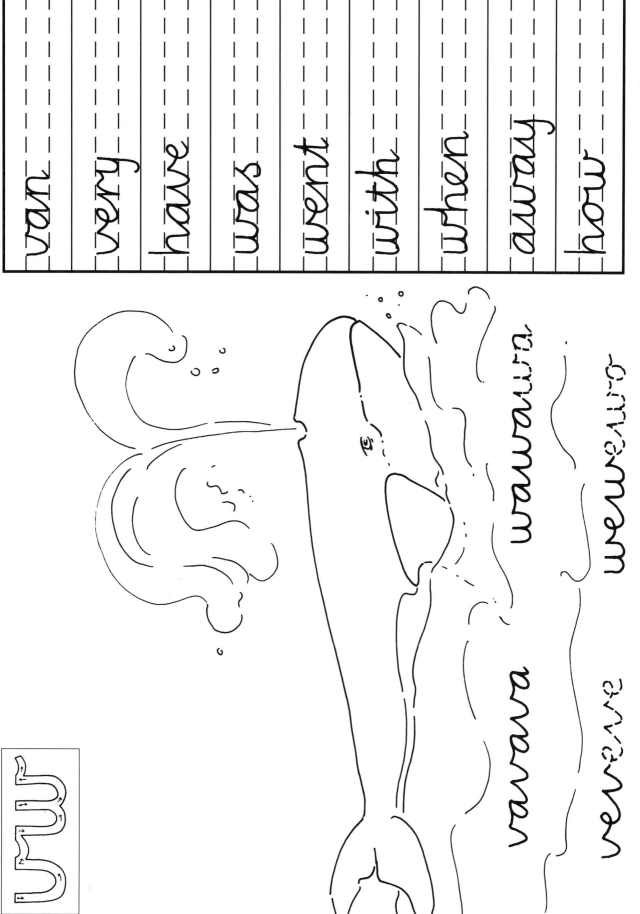

van

very

have

was

went

with

when

away

how

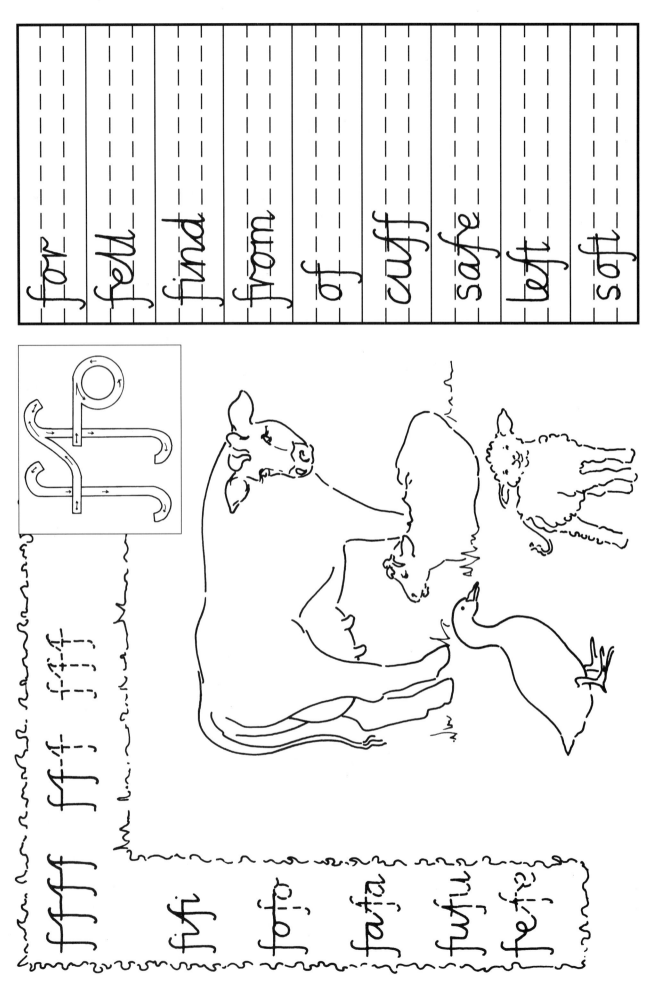

for

fell

find

from

of

cuff

safe

left

soft

ffff ffff fff

fi fi

fo fo

fa fa

fu fu

fe fe

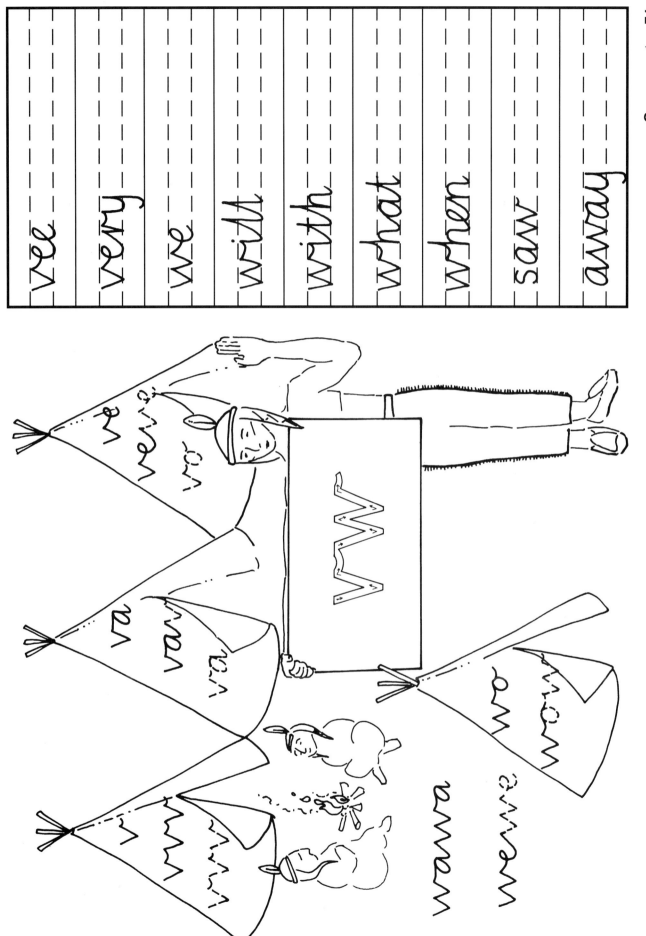

vee
very
we
will
with
what
when
saw
away

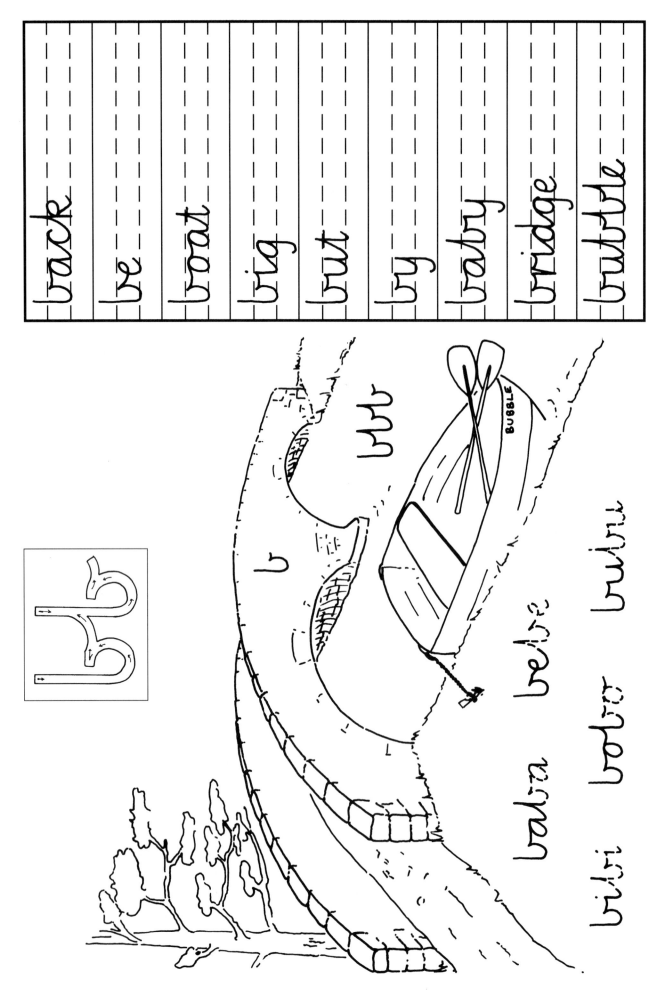

track

be

boat

big

but

by

baby

bridge

bubble

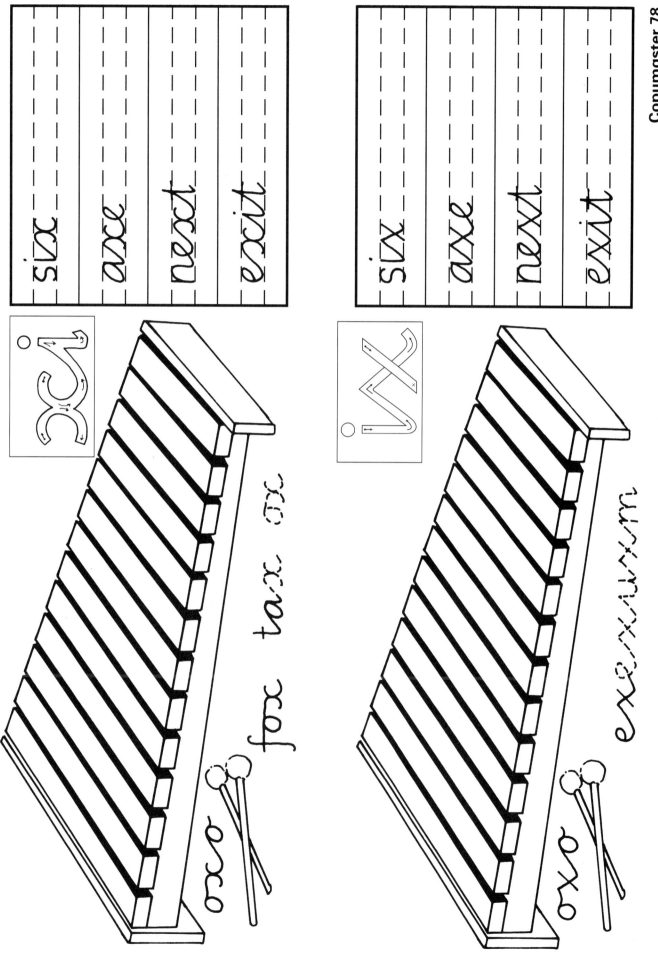

six

axe

next

exit

six

axe

next

exit

fox tax ox

exexaxexm

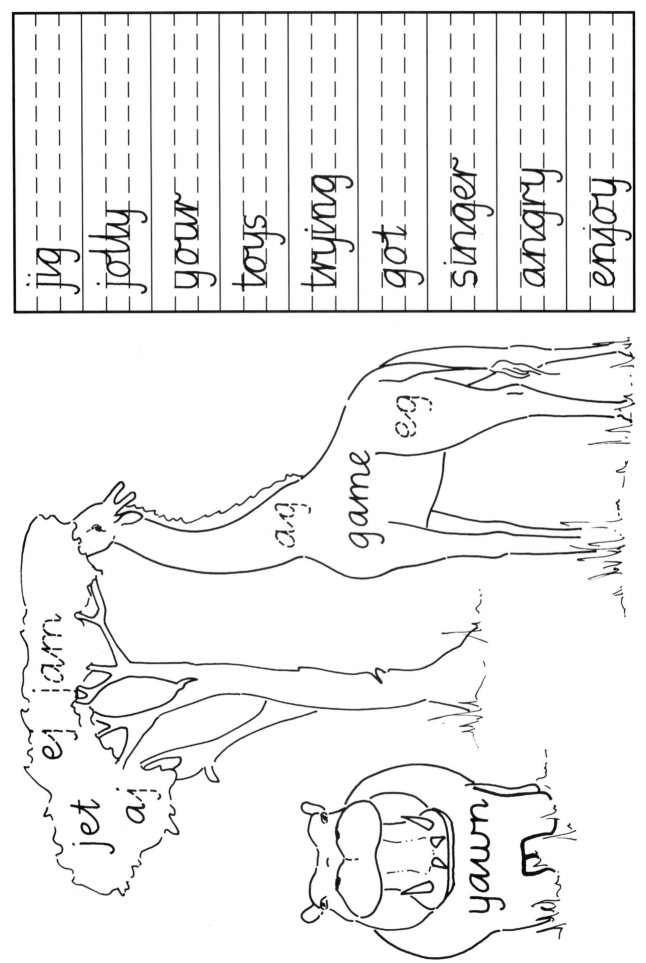

jig

jolly

your

toys

trying

got

singer

angry

enjoy

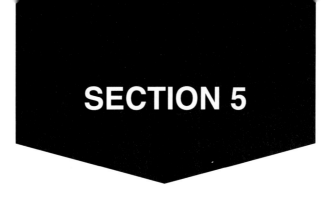

SECTION 5

HANDWRITING AND SPELLING

This section requires children to look closely at the construction of words. The words selected are those which help children to see how words are built, to learn essential words and some difficult constructions, and to spark an interest in words for their own sake.

Alternative letter forms were covered in Sections 3 and 4 but by this section only one form of each letter could be used. The letter shapes used here are fast to write, have flowing movements, develop easily from their unjoined form and are easy for children to adopt and control. Our own muscle memory may find some of the shapes awkward because for years we have written words automatically without giving their formation a thought. These letter forms here are ones which will provide a firm basis from which children can develop a mature, personal writing style.

The copymasters give children practice in joining letters to form one word at a time. Children will benefit from writing the word on their table or desk top with the index finger of their writing hand before writing on the copymaster. The words can also be practised with a range of writing implements on a variety of different textures as well as in the more practical ways suggested in Section 2.

Copymasters 80 and 81: Building words 1 and 2
With these copymasters, children learn to build words letter by letter. On each line letters are added or exchanged requiring children to look carefully at the structure of the word and the kinds of joins required. Writing the words on a ladder draws attention to the way words grow. The page can be cut into sections so that children can work from a single word list and ladder at any one time. Ask children to collect other words they can build in a similar way trying, wherever possible, to make complete words on each line and to exchange only one letter, prefix or suffix at a time.

Copymaster 82: Sh and ch words
These words are built in chunks, adding a group of letters to the digraph or the digraph to a group of letters. Each of the joins are ones commonly used with these digraphs. this page can be cut into two or four

sections are required. Note the initial form of 's' is different from 's' in the middle or at the end of a word.

Copymaster 83: Useful words
The 47 words here are taken from lists of the words most used by primary children. Children should work from only a single block of words at a time. They should practise the words first, copying them in the columns on the copymaster and then from memory. After each attempt the children should check their words for accuracy in letter formation, joins and, of course, spelling.

Copymasters 84 and 85: Double consonant words
These two pages give practice in doubling consonants as well as forming the joins which come before and after the pair of letters.

Copymaster 86: Special cases
The letter shapes for 'e' and 's' vary according to the letters which precede or follow them. There is space for the joins to be practised before the words are written. Letters 'r' and 'z' change shape on joining and again practice is given with the new letters and their common joins before the words are practised.

Copymaster 87: Time words
These frequently used words are grouped appropriately for children to make the right connections. In the 'Days of the week' and 'Months of the year' draw attention to any repeated patterns. Knowing that the endings of certain words are the same tells children that they only have the first few letters to learn not the whole word. Learning them becomes a quicker, easier and more appealing task.

Copymaster 88: Reversals
Writing these words back to front requires children to consider the joins needed to rewrite these words. Column 1 has palindromes so although the joins are unchanged children are required to think in preparation for the next two columns.

Building words

an
and
land
lands
landed
landing

all
call
fall
falls
falling
fell

tea
eat
each
teach
teaches
teacher

me
met
meet
meets
meeting
metre

Building words

ut
hut
hunt
hunter
hunters
hunted

old
fold
cold
colds
colder
coldest

on
one
bone
bones
boned
boning

coo
cook
cooks
cooked
cooking
crook

Sh and ch words

ch —
- air
- eap
- eese
- ild
- oose
- ange

ch —
- bea
- cat
- hut
- lun
- tor
- wat

sh —
- aded
- adow
- ine
- ould
- ower
- rink

sh —
- mar
- squa
- me
- fre
- fini
- thru

Useful words

away _____	into _____	over _____	this _____
back _____	like _____	said _____	very _____
came _____	live _____	some _____	went _____
come _____	look _____	take _____	what _____
down _____	made _____	that _____	when _____
from _____	next _____	then _____	will _____
have _____	once _____	they _____	with _____

about _____	their _____	because _____
after _____	there _____	myself _____
could _____	thing _____	yourself _____
other _____	three _____	whether _____

Double consonant words

bubble _____	accept _____	cuddle _____
stubble _____	accident _____	hidden _____
rabbit _____	hiccup _____	ladder _____
ribbon _____	occupy _____	middle _____
rubbed _____	occur _____	puddle _____
webbed _____	soccer _____	suddenly _____
afford _____	collar _____	common _____
effort _____	fallen _____	hammer _____
fluffy _____	really _____	mammal _____
office _____	thrill _____	shimmer _____
stuffed _____	wallet _____	simmer _____
toffee _____	yellow _____	summer _____

More double consonant words

cannot	apple	berry
dinner	happen	borrow
kennel	happy	cherry
runner	pepper	furry
tinned	puppy	mirror
tunnel	supper	sorry
assist	attack	buzzer
bossy	better	dazzle
chess	bottle	fizzy
fossil	kitten	muzzle
glass	pretty	pizza
lesson	rattle	puzzle

Special cases e and S

de	dell
	deep
oe	toe
	woe
we	went
	weave

es	less
	wishes
sl	slope
	slowly
os	lost
	loses

Special cases r = r   z = z

ra	rabbit
re	reader
ri	ribbon
ro	rockery
ru	rumour
ry	contrary

za	wizard
ze	dozen
zi	zither
zo	ozone
zu	azure
zy	crazy

Time words

morning

afternoon

evening

night

day

week

month

year

yesterday

today

tomorrow

next

Days of the week

Sunday

Monday

Tuesday

Wednesday

Thursday

Friday

Saturday

Months of the year

January

February

March

April

May

June

July

August

September

October

November

December

Reversals

Write these words back to front. What happens?

did _____ evil

ewe _____

nap _____ rats

level _____ revel

now _____

madam _____ pin

tub _____

rotor _____

saw _____ war

Write these sentences to practise the letters of the alphabet.

The quick brown fox jumps over the lazy dog.

_____

_____

Johnny asked if Mum was quite pleased with our gift of a clever zebra and onyx.

_____

_____

PRACTISING FOR FLOW AND FLUENCY

In response to the questionnaire sent out by the publishers, most of the teachers asked for items for children to copy; Section 6 covers this request. Items range from proverbs of very few words to poems by children in my class and those by adult poets. There are also some jokes and amusing pieces to cheer the reluctant learner.

The pieces, however short or long, should be used both for 'best' copy and to encourage children to write with speed and fluency. If children write a page for both 'best' and speed and then compare the difference they can make critical judgements about the quality of copy needed when writing for different purposes. On some days give time limits to encourage faster movements but remind children that however fast they try to write the end result must be clear, clean and legible.

Many of the items included for copying are short for a good reason. In my classroom children usually copied a short piece of handwriting writing each day rather than be subjected to one long period per week. The shortness of the pieces prevented children from becoming bored with practising their writing. They also meant that children could have daily reinforcement on how to shape and join their letters in a way which was interesting but did not take too much time.

All the pieces are set in frames so they can be cut and shared between children. If you photocopy them on to card or mount the paper copymasters before laminating them or covering them with self-adhesive transparent film, the collection will last a long time.

Copymaster 89: Christmas
A Christmas shopping list and a thank you letter are both essential elements of the festive season. These two are not only for copying but also to serve as examples for children's own creative writing.

Copymaster 90: Stuff and nonsense
Stuff and nonsense is just that – awful jokes and plays on words. Why not use these as the beginning of a class collection. Children can write out other ones they collect and stick them in the book.

Copymaster 91: Proverbs
These short pithy sayings express well-known truths or facts. Children can write them out several times

underneath each other trying to pick up speed each time without losing legibility. Encourage children to say the proverb in their heads as they write, it will help them to write faster because they will be anticipating the movements to be made for specific words. It will also make them familiar with sayings which are part of our language heritage. Proverbs are also excellent subjects for discussion on a number of levels.

Copymaster 92: Limericks
Limericks are said to be England's own original verse form yet its origins may possibly go back to Aristophenes. Certainly the British Museum has a 14th century one and Shakespeare and Ben Johnson used them. The first book of limericks was published in London in 1821 although the word limerick was not coined until the end of the century.

Limericks are droll and the rhythms are ones children find easy to write. They use its rhythm to increase their speed of writing because they can anticipate the word which comes next. They can easily remember one or two lines of a limerick at a time which also increases their speed of writing. Repetition is strong in limericks and allows children to practise particular groups of letters. Both the limericks included here were written by children in my school and printed in one of our publications.

Copymasters 93–5: Poems
Poems by well-known authors fill these three pages. These are worthy of a child's best writing and could be used to begin their own personal anthology. These are not for writing in haste but for writing for its own sake and to enjoy the work of these poets.

Copymaster 96: More poems
The Japanese hold strictly to the meaning of each line of a haiku but in England we apply a looser meaning. These haiku in 5, 7, 5 syllabic form hold a snapshot, a moment of wonder in the middle of a cold winter. They can be copied into a child's poetry anthology and used as a springboard for writing in the same form. The other poem will, I hope, give pleasure to the child writing it as he or she tries hard with the craft of handwriting.

Copymaster 97: Old number rhymes
This sheet uses traditional number rhymes to give children practice in writing numbers as words.

103 Fenton Street
Benham

Dear Grandma,

Thankyou very much
for the hiking boots you
gave me for Christmas.
We went for a walk
and I wore my new boots.
They were great.
I hope you had a nice
Christmas.

Lots of love from
Chris x x

In my Christmas stocking
I would like:

a teddy bear
a cartoon video
some felt pens
a toy chest
a computer game
a patchwork jumper
a pair of hiking boots
a pair of dungarees
and a good book.

Why did the one-eyed chicken cross the road?

To get to the Bird's Eye shop.

Why do storks stand on one leg?

Because if they lifted both legs up they'd fall over.

What is black and comes out of the ground at 100 miles an hour?

A mole on a motorbike.

Why did the orange stop rolling up the hill?

Because it ran out of juice.

What is orange and comes out of the ground at 500 miles an hour?

A jet-propelled carrot.

What is a cat nap?

A sleeping kitten.

What is a knap-sack?

A sleeping bag.

Actions speak louder than words.	Well begun is half done.	A friend in need is a friend indeed.
You must learn to walk before you can run.	First things first.	Better to be safe than sorry.
There is no time like the present.	Do as you would be done by.	What is done cannot be undone.
It is the first step that is difficult.	Every little helps.	Waste not want not.

Limericks

There was an old man called
Tom Crockett,
Who went to the moon in a rocket.
The rocket went bang,
His head went clang
And ended up in his pocket.

Francis Lane (aged 10)

There once was a boy called Mark,
Who went to the zoo for a lark.
But the zoo caught on fire
So he sat on a wire,
Now Mark is a bright little spark.

Louise Raymond (aged 11)

THE END

When I was One,
I was just begun.

When I was Two,
I was nearly new.

When I was Four,
I was not much more.

When I was Five,
I was just alive.

But now I am Six,
I'm clever as clever
So I think I'll be six now
for ever and ever.

WHAT IS THE SUN?

the Sun is an orange dinghy

sailing across a calm sea

it is a gold coin

dropped down a drain in Heaven

the Sun is a yellow beach ball

kicked high into the summer sky

it is a red thumb-print

on a sheet of pale blue paper

the Sun is a milk bottle's gold top

floating in a puddle

SUMMER SUN

Yes,

the sun shines

bright

in the summer,

and the breeze

is soft

as a sigh.

Yes,

the days are

long

in the summer,

and the sun

is king

of the sky.

POEMS by Judith Nichols

TIGER

Tiger, eyes dark with
half-remembered forest night
stalks an empty cage.

SEASON SONG

Spring stirs slowly, shuffles, hops;
Summer dances close behind.
Autumn is a jostly crowd
but Winter creeps into your mind.

BIKING

Fingers grip,
toes curl;
head down,
wheels whirl.

Hair streams,
fields race;
ears sting,
winds chase.

Breathe deep,
troubles gone;
just feel
windsong.

HAIKU

It's really snowing
I'm bursting with excitement
To build a snowman.
                Jon (aged 8)

Icy white crystals
of snow, falling on my hand
dissolve straight away.
                Simon (aged 8)

A freezing morning
neckless blue tits huddle
together for warmth.
                Helen Hadley

ROBBERS

A pair of cheeky silent starlings
rob the golden winter jasmine,
their beaks too full of yellow blooms
to make their usual chattering.
                Helen Hadley

As I was going to St Ives,
I met a man with seven wives;
Each wife had seven sacks,
Each sack had seven cats,
Each cat had seven kits;
Kits, cats, sacks, wives,
How many were there going to St Ives?

One, two, three, four, five,
Once I caught a fish alive,
Six, seven, eight, nine, ten,
Then I let him go again.

Thirty days has September,
April, June and November;
All the rest have thirty-one
Excepting February alone,
And that has twenty-eight days clear
And twenty-nine in each leap year.

SECTION 7

BORDERS

A range of borders fills this section of copymasters, some with just borders, others with seasonal motifs and others divided into sections for children to complete with smaller quotations. They provide ready made presentation sheets for children to colour after they have completed writing on them.

The idea behind this section is to imprint in children that their writing does not have to be presented baldly on a plain piece of paper – unless it is required by the nature of the task – it can be set off by suitable illustrations both large and small.

Special reference is made to copymasters in Section 6 but obviously the suitability of these pieces will depend on the age of the child and his or her writing competence.

Copymasters 98 and 99
These borders allow children to practise basic strokes, and lets them see that handwriting can be used for making patterns themselves, here as a decorative border.

Copymasters 100–103
This group depicts the four seasons, each using a different style of decoration but reflecting the elements. Wes Magee's poems (Copymaster 94) are ideal for the summer scene, the haiku (Copymaster 96) are more suited to the snowman and their call of winter whilst the poem 'Robbers' pre-empts spring.

The copymasters should be a springboard for the children to develop their own ideas on ways of reflecting their own poems and those by others whose work they enjoy. Encourage children to use these pages to start their own poetry anthology.

Copymaster 104
Christmas (spiritual), will be useful for notices, letters, advertisements and programmes. After children have completed their writing the sheets can be enlarged on the photocopier if need be and hand coloured by the children for use on the school premises. Christmas cards and prayers are also suitable for this sheet whilst the thank you letter (Copymaster 89) would sit well on the winter copymaster (Copymaster 103).

Copymaster 105
This copymaster could be the setting for nursery rhymes and children's verses. It also lends itself to the jokes on 'stuff and nonsense' (Copymaster 90), and A.A. Milne's poems (Copymaster 93).

Copymaster 106
Two spaces are provided here. Judith Nicholl's poems (Copymaster 95), A.A. Milne's (Copymaster 93), some of the number rhymes, (Copymaster 97) and limericks (Copymaster 92) are all suitable for this page.

Copymasters 107 and 108
These two copymasters provide the setting for a number of short pieces which can be written at one sitting or over a period of a few days. Short pieces do not take long to write and tend to have a stronger focus of attention upon them than might be given to a longer piece.

Name _____

Name _____

Name _____

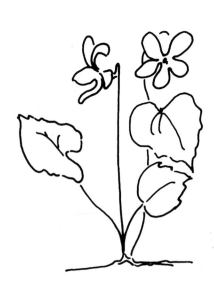

Name _____

Copymaster 101

Name _____

Name _____

Name _____

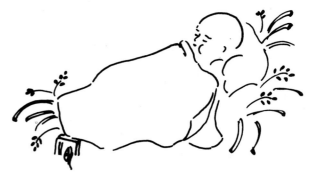

Name _____

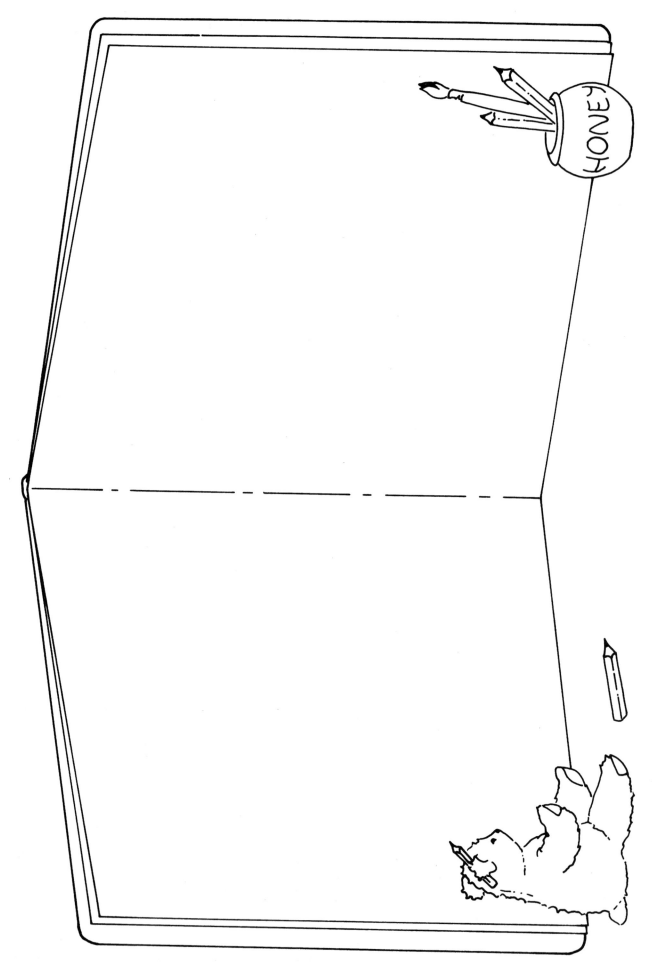

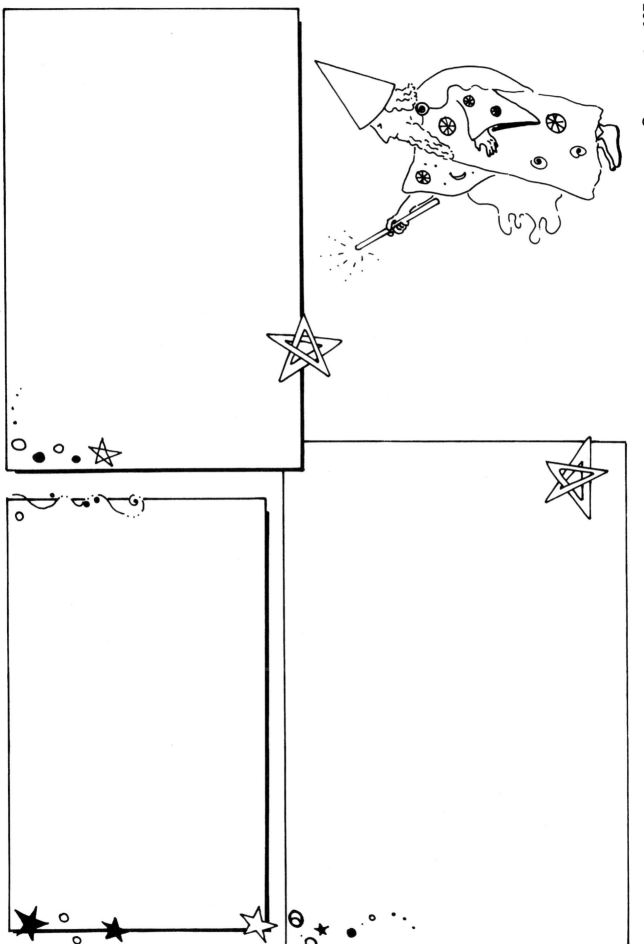

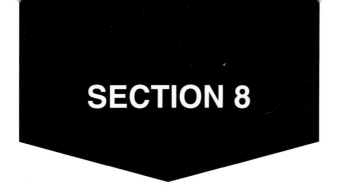

SECTION 8

FLICK LETTERS, LINES AND CHARTS

Copymasters 109–117: Flick letters

The number of cards to make up a set varies from 3 to 7. Cut the copymaster across the width before carefully cutting the letters off the strip. The measurements of the card have to be exact so it is important to cut precisely on the line. Assemble the cards for any one letter so that the left edges meet exactly and then staple them together. Holding the stapled edge in the left hand and flicking the right hand edges will reveal how the letter is formed.

Copymasters 118–120: Lines

These copymasters are for use as guides under blank paper but can also be used as lined writing paper if need be. 118 has 15 mm line spaces, 119 has 15 line spaces with training lines for height differentials, 120 has 8 mm lines.

Copymasters 121–123: Alphabet charts

These sheets can either be trimmed and stuck together to make one wall chart or cut into strips to make a continuous alphabet strip at child height. Variant letter forms are included so that the charts can be adapted to your own use.

1.   5.   4.   1.

2.   6.   3.   2.

3.   5.   4.   1.

4.   6.   3.   2.

Flick letters

Flick letters

1.	5.	4.	1.
2.	6.	3.	2.
3.	5.	4.	1.
4.	5.	3.	2.

Flick letters

Flick letters

1.

2.

3.

4.

5.

6.

5.

6.

4.

3.

4.

3.

1.

2.

1.

2.

1.	5.	4.	1.
2.	6.	3.	2.
3.	5.	4.	1.
4.	6.	3.	2.

Flick letters

1.	5.
2.	6.
3.	5.
4.	6.
4.	1.
3.	2.
1.	3.
2.	2.

Flick letters

Flick letters

1.	5.
2.	6.
3.	4.
4.	3.
5.	5.
6.	6.
1.	4.
2.	3.
1.	1.
2.	2.

Flick letters

Lines

A a	B b	C c	D d
E e	F f	G g	H h
I i	J j	K k	L l

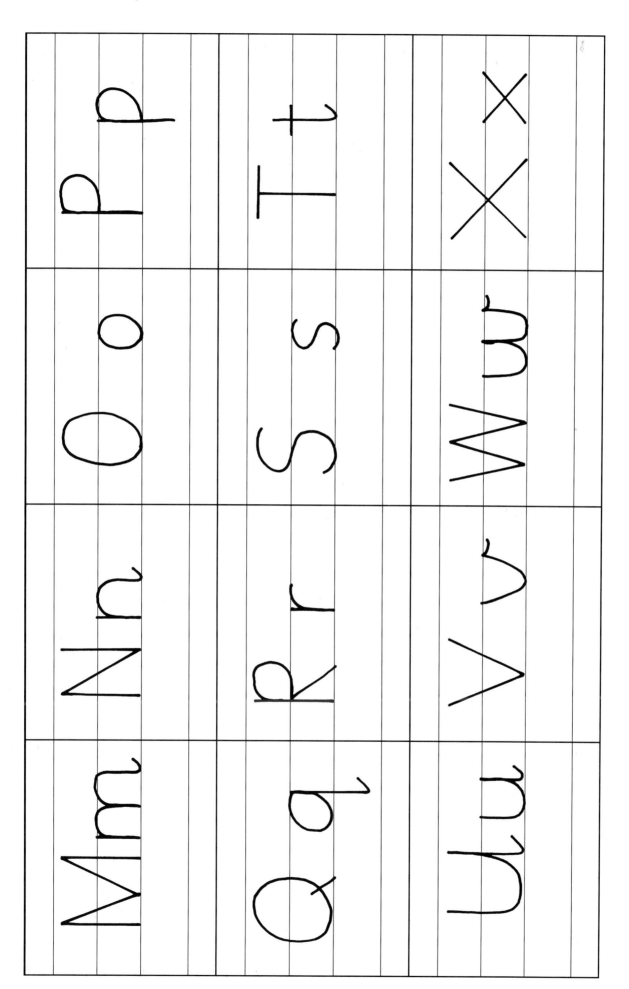

Mm	Nn	Oo	Pp
Qq	Rr	Ss	Tt
Uu	Vv	Ww	Xx

Alphabet charts

Alphabet charts